Getting Organized *for your* New Baby

3rd Edition

Maureen Bard
and
Christine Zuchora-Walske

THIRD EYE

GETTING ORGANIZED FOR YOUR NEW BABY

First published in India by

THIRD EYE
An Imprint of
PENTAGON PRESS
A-38, Hauz Khas, New Delhi-110016 (India)
Phones: 011-41656996/7/8, 41517091 • Telefax: 011-41656997
email: pentagonpress@airtelbroadband.in
Website: www.pentagon-press.com

PUBLISHED BY ARRANGEMENT WITH
MEADOWBROOK PRESS
5451 SMETANA DRIVE, MINNETONKA, MINNESOTA 55343

Maureen Bard and Christine Zuchora-Walske

First Published: 2005
Reprinted: 2007

ISBN - 81-8274-971-9

Printed by New Elegant Printers, New Delhi-110064

Dedication

To Maureen Bard and
Tony Zuchora-Walske,
without whose gifts this
book would not exist.

Contents

Introduction

Congratulations on your pregnancy! And kudos to you for having the good sense to get organized for your baby *now*.

I learned the hard way that when it comes to babies, organization is your friend. For most of my life, I sneered at planners. Hating to miss an adventure, I just followed life where it led me. Then Hurricane Tony (my one-year-old son) blew in two weeks early. His crib wasn't assembled. We hadn't researched newborn medical procedures. All his clothes were too big. And—horrors—we had no baby wipes! These and other tactical errors had my husband, Ron, and I scrambling to get our act together during Tony's first days, when we should have been resting as much as possible.

If I have any say in the matter, new parenthood will go a lot more smoothly for you than it did for me. Using hindsight, the wisdom of other parents, and exhaustive research, I've updated *Getting Organized for Your New Baby* for the new millennium.

This third edition builds on the practical, interactive, easy-to-use features of Maureen Bard's classic road map through pregnancy. In it you'll still find essential information on getting pregnant, prenatal health, childbirth preparation, baby gear, household management, financial planning, childcare, celebrations, and life with baby—now infused with the latest, greatest knowledge about pregnancy and parenting. I've also added key facts and resources to help busy (and possibly bewildered) parents-to-be in their constant decision-making.

I hope this book helps you keep your stress level low and your enjoyment high as you settle into parenthood. Now—sit down, put your feet up, grab a pencil, and get organized!

Christine Zuchora-Walske

Chapter One

Maybe Baby?

Things to Think about before You Conceive

Preparing for a baby begins well before you get pregnant. A baby will affect many areas of your life. It's important to consider the changes a baby will bring and to prepare yourself and your family for the transition.

Relationships

- Do you and your partner have a stable relationship?
- Do you and your partner share a common parenting philosophy?
- Have you considered how a new baby will affect your relationship with your partner?
- How might a new baby affect any child(ren) you may already have?

Health

- Do you have any medical conditions that may affect pregnancy? (See Medical History Organizer on page 28.)
- Is age a factor for either partner?
- Are you getting enough folic acid? The U.S. Public Health Service recommends that all women who could become pregnant get 400 micrograms (0.4 milligrams) of folic acid every day to prevent neural tube defects (serious birth defects of the spine and brain, like spina bifida and anencephaly).
- Does your doctor recommend you or your partner:
  - Stop smoking?
  - Limit or cease alcohol consumption?
  - Adjust your diet or fitness regimen?
  - Make any changes to create a healthier home or work environment?
  - Complete any necessary medical or dental procedures or treatments?
  - Update vaccinations or injections?
  - Change medications (either prescription or over-the-counter)?
  - Consider genetic screening? (See page 67.)

Finances

- Can you afford a child? (See page 146.)
  - What is a comfortable minimum income?
  - What is a comfortable minimum savings?

- If you experience prenatal disability, a difficult postpartum recovery, or a chronically ill infant, can you afford to become a one-income household? For how long?
- What costs will you incur if you have a new baby? (See the following questions.)

- Household expenses
  - Will you need a larger home?
  - Will housing restrictions require you to move?
  - Will you have to remodel your home?
  - How much will your day-to-day household expenses (such as groceries and utilities) increase?
- Transportation needs
  - Will you need to buy a vehicle?
  - Will you have to purchase car seats?
  - Will your auto insurance increase?
- Health insurance
  - Will you have to purchase health insurance or expand your current coverage?
- Childcare
  - Will you need full- or part-time childcare? (See pages 178–183 to evaluate childcare options.)
  - How much will a childcare provider cost?
- Employment
  - Will either you or your partner change career paths? (See page 150 to evaluate work-family scenarios.)
  - If so, how will this affect your income?

Career

- If both you and your partner plan to continue full-time careers, will either of you take a leave of absence?
- If you or your partner plans to work part-time following your baby's birth, will you have to find a new job or inquire about flexible scheduling or job-sharing?
- Will you or your partner quit working to care for your baby?
- Will you or your partner change careers?
- Will your job(s) require traveling after your baby is born?
- Will either of you be able to work at home?

Insurance

- Healthcare coverage (See page 153.)
  - Is pregnancy covered in your policy?
  - What pregnancy-related items (genetic testing, infertility testing and treatment, prenatal care, vaginal delivery, cesarean section, hospitalization) are covered, and at what percentages?
  - What pregnancy-related items and preexisting conditions are not covered in your healthcare policy?
  - Are your current healthcare benefits sufficient for a baby?
- Do you need additional life or disability insurance?

Timing

- Is the timing of your pregnancy important?
- Is there a less-stressful period during your yearly work schedule?
- Is help more readily available during specific times?
- Can you maximize your insurance deductible by timing your pregnancy?

Getting Pregnant

To get pregnant, you must have sexual intercourse near the time you ovulate. Ovulation is when an ovary releases one or more eggs into a fallopian tube. The timing of ovulation can vary from menstrual cycle to menstrual cycle. You can try to determine when you ovulate and increase your chances of conceiving by charting your body's monthly changes and your sexual activity. Charting involves:

- Noting the first day of your menstrual period.
- Taking your basal body temperature.
- Examining your cervical mucus.
- Noting when you had sexual intercourse.

Menstrual Cycle

During every menstrual cycle, your uterus builds up an internal lining of tissue called endometrium in preparation for ovulation. If an egg becomes fertilized, it implants in the tissue and begins to grow into a fetus. An unfertilized egg doesn't implant, and the tissue sloughs off in a process called menstruation.

Noting the first day of each menstrual period gives you an obvious starting date for each menstrual cycle. After you've recorded the starting day for a few months, you can see how long your menstrual cycle usually lasts, which is a first step toward predicting ovulation.

Mark the first day of your menstrual period on the chart on page 7. (Make a few photocopies of the chart, so you can monitor your fertility for a few cycles.)

Basal Body Temperature (BBT)

Your basal body temperature is the temperature of your body at rest. Your BBT probably ranges from 97.2°F to about 97.7°F before ovulation. When you ovulate, your BBT rises 0.5°F to 1°F and remains elevated for several days (usually until your next period). If you conceive, your temperature stays elevated throughout your pregnancy.

Charting your BBT over a few months helps you see whether there's a pattern to your cycle. The information can help you pinpoint when you ovulated, because a sustained increase in your BBT shows that ovulation has occurred. You may note your BBT spiking on other days, but unless it stays elevated, you probably haven't yet ovulated.

Use a basal thermometer (available at drugstores) to take your BBT. A basal thermometer shows the incremental temperature changes that a regular thermometer can't. To get an accurate reading, take your BBT upon waking each morning, and try to wake up at the same time. Any activity raises your BBT, so take your BBT before you get out of bed, brush your teeth, get dressed, or otherwise start your day. If you don't take your BBT at a regular time and upon waking, any pattern you find may be inaccurate.

Record your BBT on the chart on page 7. Start recording on the first day of your menstrual period.

Cervical Mucus

Cervical mucus is a secretion triggered by the hormone estrogen. It's important for conception because it keeps sperm alive, protecting them from vaginal acidity and carrying them to the fallopian tube for fertilization with an egg.

During a menstrual cycle the ovaries produce varying amounts of estrogen, so cervical mucus ranges in amount, consistency, color, and fertile quality. The changes in mucus usually follow this pattern:

Infertile

Dry or Light Moisture

For three to five days after menstruation, a small amount of mucus (if any) appears. It's clear or slightly white, and it dries immediately when touched. Overall, you feel dry.

Sticky or Gummy

During the following two to three days, the mucus feels sticky and it resists a little or crumbles when rubbed between your fingertips. Its color ranges from clear to white. You still feel dry.

Fertile

Creamy, Milky, Lotion-like

During the next two to four days, more mucus appears, and it's wet. It may look thick and creamy or like lotion. It may form peaks on your fingertips when pulled apart, or it may be thinner and milky. It's white or yellow. You feel wet.

Egg White–like

For the next one to five days, the mucus looks and feels like egg white. It's slippery and very stretchy. It's clear or iridescent. You feel extremely wet and are approaching ovulation.

Infertile

Dry, Moist, or Sticky

At this time, a drop in estrogen and a surge of progesterone following ovulation change the mucus. It can be dry, moist, or sticky and remains so until you menstruate and the pattern begins again. Any mucus dries quickly when it's touched. Its color ranges from clear to white. You feel dry.

Charting your cervical mucus for a few months helps you recognize your body's patterns and determine when you're about to ovulate. Use the chart on page 7 to note the appearance of your cervical mucus each day. For example, write *P* (period), *S* (sticky), *C* (creamy), or *E* (egg white). Note, too, how you feel overall: *D* (dry), *M* (moist), or *W* (wet).

Basal Body Temperature and Cervical Mucus Chart

Name: ______________________ Dates covered: ____/____/____ to ____/____/____

Cycle Day	1	2	3	4	5	6	7	8	9	10	11	12	13	14	15	16	17	18	19	20	21	22	23	24	25	26	27	28	29	30	31	32	33	34	35	36	37	38	39	40	41	42	43	44	45
Day of week																																													
Date																																													
Time																																													
99.1																																													
99.0																																													
98.9																																													
98.8																																													
98.7																																													
98.6																																													
98.5																																													
98.4																																													
98.3																																													
98.2																																													
98.1																																													
98.0																																													
97.9																																													
97.8																																													
97.7																																													
97.6																																													
97.5																																													
97.4																																													
97.3																																													
97.2																																													
97.1																																													
97.0																																													
96.9																																													
Intercourse																																													
Cervical mucus																																													
Overall																																													

Other Methods for Predicting Ovulation

Cervical Position

As ovulation approaches, the cervix rises, and the muscle softens and opens to let sperm pass. At peak fertility, the cervix's opening is about 1.5 centimeters wide. After ovulation, the cervix drops, and the muscle is firm and closed. In fact, the cervix is so low, you can touch it.

Mittelschmerz

Mittelschmerz is lower abdominal discomfort caused by ovulation. Only 20 percent of women experience mittelschmerz, which can range from mild aches to twinges of pain that can last from a few minutes to a few hours.

Ovulation Predictor Kits (OPKs)

Ovulation predictor kits spot an increase in luteinizing hormone (LH), which prompts ovulation, twenty-four to thirty-six hours before ovulation. They're available without a prescription at drugstores and grocery stores, and they usually cost fifteen to fifty dollars. OPKs are easier to use and often more accurate than charting your BBT. For maximum accuracy, follow the kit's instructions exactly.

Sexual Intercourse

Charting your body's monthly changes helps you predict ovulation and schedule a window of time during which sexual intercourse will most likely result in pregnancy. With the help of fertile cervical mucus, sperm can live for six days (usually two to three days) inside the uterus and fallopian tubes, but an egg can't survive more than one day after ovulation. This means that if you have sex often during the five days before ovulation and one day afterward, you increase your chances of conceiving.

Additional Questions to Ask Your Healthcare Provider

(See also questions under Health on page 2.)

- Does our former birth control method affect conception?
- Does duration of contraceptive use affect fertility?
- Do we need to wait after quitting our birth control method before trying to conceive?
- Should I use douches and lubricants?
- Should I lie in a particular position after intercourse?
- Should I avoid any specific medications, environments, clothing, or activities while trying to conceive?
- Besides vitamins, what other nutrients should I take before conceiving?
- Can I take megavitamins while trying to conceive?
- Do some foods increase the chance of conception?
- Can I diet while trying to conceive?
- Are some sexual positions better than others for conception?
- Are there methods that can help us conceive a boy or girl?
- Can I conceive while nursing?
- Does a past abortion affect my chances of conceiving?
- Do previous miscarriages affect fertility?
- What chronic illnesses can affect fertility? Why?
- Does stress hinder conception?
- How long should I wait before conceiving again after a cesarean?
- How long will it take to get pregnant after surgical sterilization is reversed?
- How soon after quitting smoking can I try to get pregnant?
- I want to start an exercise program now that I can continue through pregnancy. What do you recommend?
- Should we steer clear of the hot tub while trying to get pregnant?
- Other questions: ______________________________

Chapter Two

Prenatal Planning

Obstetrical Care

Types of Obstetrical Care Providers

You have several options when choosing an obstetrical care provider. The following list groups caregivers by education, training, philosophy, and availability. Your philosophy, personality, and type of pregnancy will influence your decision. So will your insurance coverage and delivery center. Make sure the caregiver you choose is covered by your insurance plan and is affiliated with your delivery center of choice.

Medical Doctors

Obstetrician-Gynecologist (Ob-gyn)
- Received a Doctor of Medicine (MD) or Doctor of Osteopathy (DO) degree with an additional three or more years of specialty training in obstetrics and gynecology.
- May have passed board-certification exams administered by the American Board of Obstetrics and Gynecology (ABOG).

Perinatologist
- Is an ob-gyn with additional training in high-risk pregnancies.
- Practices only in major medical centers in urban areas.

Family Physician
- Received an MD or DO with an additional two or more years of specialty training in family medicine.
- Frequently consults with specialists in high-risk pregnancies.
- May not include maternity care in practice.

General Practitioner
- Received an MD or DO.
- Frequently consults with ob-gyns.

Advanced Practice Nurses

Certified Nurse-Midwife (CNM)
- Is a registered nurse (RN) who has completed one or more years of additional training in midwifery and has been certified according to the requirements of the American College of Nurse-Midwives (ACNM).

- Focuses on normal healthcare during the childbearing years, psychosocial and emotional aspects of childbearing, parent education, prevention of and screening for possible problems, and newborn care.
- Provides care for women with uncomplicated pregnancies and births.
- Works with physicians and has hospital or birth center affiliation.

Women's Health Nurse Practitioner
- Is an RN with advanced training who has met the requirements set by the state government and nursing board.
- Provides prenatal and postpartum care but doesn't care for women in labor.
- Often works in a clinic or group with one or more physicians or midwives.

Midwives

Many terms are used to describe the different types of midwives available in North America. The following list explains the most common titles for midwives. Note that the types overlap. For example, a direct-entry midwife may be either a licensed midwife or a lay midwife.

Certified Nurse-Midwife (CNM)
See page 12.

Certified Midwife (CM)
- Is educated in the discipline of midwifery and has been certified according to the requirements of the ACNM.
- The term *certified midwife* is also used in some states to indicate certification by the state midwifery organization.

Licensed Midwife (LM)
- Is licensed to practice in a particular state or province.
- May be called a certified midwife in some states.

Certified Professional Midwife (CPM)
- Is educated in the discipline of midwifery and has met the standards for certification set by the North American Registry of Midwives (NARM).
- Practices outside a hospital.

Direct-Entry Midwife (DEM)
- Is educated in the discipline of midwifery through self-study, apprenticeship, a midwifery school, or a college- or university-based program distinct from the discipline of nursing.
- Practices primarily outside hospitals.

Lay Midwife

- Is uncertified or unlicensed.
- Is educated primarily through self-study or apprenticeship rather than through formal schooling.
- May be called a traditional midwife, traditional birth attendant, granny midwife, or independent midwife.

Complementary and Alternative Healthcare Providers

Naturopathic Doctor (ND)

- Specializes in noninvasive natural childbirth; doesn't use drugs or pharmaceuticals and doesn't perform major surgical procedures.
- Has participated in a specialized course of study and received degrees in naturopathy.
- May be required to pass a national or state board exam to obtain licensure, and a state board of examiners may review the practice.
- Refers patients to medical practitioners for diagnosis or treatment when appropriate.

Locating a Caregiver

You can find a caregiver using the following resources:

- Labor-delivery or birth center of a hospital or clinic: Phone your chosen hospital or clinic and find out what caregivers have privileges there.
- Prenatal organizations focused on a particular method or philosophy, such as Lamaze International
- Regional prenatal organizations, such as the Minnesota Birth Network
- Health insurance provider directory: Your selection might be confined to a specific group of healthcare providers.
- Friends with children: Parents usually have strong feelings about their maternity caregivers. Consider both positive and negative comments.
- Online caregiver locators, such as Find a Midwife at http://www.acnm.org, the directory of natural birth specialists at http://www.birthpartners.com, or Find a Physician at http://www.acog.org.
- County health association or board of health
- *The Official ABMS Directory of Board Certified Medical Specialists* (available at your local library)
- Local chapters of caregiver associations, such as ACNM, the American Medical Association (AMA), or the American College of Obstetricians and Gynecologists (ACOG)
- Childbirth education classmates
- Teaching hospitals

- Telephone directory yellow pages, under *Physicians*, *Obstetricians*, *Midwives*, and/or *Birth Centers*

Caregiver Evaluator

The following checklist will help you evaluate a caregiver. Take your birth plan (page 81) to the interview and ask the caregiver about each point. Record each response as either agreeing (+) or disagreeing (-) with your birth plan. Mark a slash (/) for valid responses that are neither (+) nor (-) or that require additional thought or discussion. Be aware that your caregiver may be reluctant to provide detailed responses to questions about hypothetical situations.

A physician or nurse-midwife most likely belongs to a group of caregivers who share on-call duties. The caregiver who attends your pregnancy may not be the person who attends your delivery. For this reason, you may want to choose a caregiver group according to general approach (for example, midwife versus ob-gyn), and you may want to meet the other caregivers in the group.

Caregiver's name: ____________________
Telephone number(s): ____________________
E-mail address: ____________________
Appointment date and time: ____________________
Referred by: ____________________

	Response	Comments or Questions
Labor Procedures/Practices		
Role of the partner		
Position during labor		
Onset of labor		
Hydration		
Vaginal exams		
Monitoring techniques		
Comfort measures		
Pain relief		
Enhancing or speeding labor		
Emptying bladder		

	Response	Comments or Questions
Birth Procedures/Practices		
Position		
Bed for labor		
Expulsion techniques		
Hastening birth		
Emergency/unexpected events		
Cleanliness of the perineum		
Care of the perineum		
Afterbirth Procedures/Practices		
Delivery of the placenta		
Cord cutting		
Baby Care		
Airway		
Warmth		
Immediate care		
Eye care		
Vaccinations		
Vitamin K		
Blood tests		
First feedings		
Contact with baby		
Circumcision		
Discharge of mother		
Discharge of baby		
Qualifications		
Education		
Postgraduate training		
Professional credentials		
Certification		
Memberships		
Licensure		
Experience—number of:		
Vaginal births		
Cesarean births		

	Response	Comments or Questions
Vaginal births after cesarean (VBACs)		
High-risk births		
Births with epidurals or intrathecal narcotics		
Births with other medications		
Birth Site Affiliations		
Hospitals		
Birth centers		
Home birth		
Personal Care		
Amount of contact:		
During prenatal exams		
During labor		
During delivery		
During postpartum		
Individual or group practice:		
Number of colleagues		
Other on-site resources:		
Midwife		
Nurse practitioner		
Dietitian		
Physical therapist		
Counselor or social worker		
Laboratory		
Prenatal Examinations		
Frequency		
Who will perform		
Visitors allowed:		
Partner		
Child(ren)		
Birth partner		
Other		
Outline of procedures		

	Response	Comments or Questions
Birth Backup Procedures		
Chance of colleague attending		
Emergency backup		
Education Recommendations		
Childbirth classes		
Breastfeeding classes		
Resource materials		
Support groups		
Exercise classes		
Newborn care classes		
Office Procedures and Fees		
Estimated costs		
Payment schedule		
Sliding fee available		
Insurance claim filing procedures		
Average waiting time for office visit		
Accessibility to:		
Workplace		
Home		
Childcare		
Office environment:		
Friendly, respectful, helpful staff		
Clean		
Comfortable		
Play area for siblings		
Other Comments:		

Selecting a Birth Site

You should consider a number of factors when deciding where to have your baby. The safety of you and your baby is the most important factor, but you should also think of your comfort and the amount of control you and your partner would like to have. Use the questions in this section to choose a birth site that will provide a safe and positive experience.

Where Will Your Baby Be Born?

- Hospital
- Birth center
- Clinic
- Home (See page 25.)

Birth Site Evaluation

Site name: ____________________
Address: ____________________
Website: ____________________
Information provided by: ____________________
Title: ____________________
Phone: ____________________
E-mail: ____________________

Use the following questions to evaluate any hospital, birth center, or clinic you're considering for your delivery. Ask these questions while touring the facility or during a private (and possibly paid) appointment with a staff member.

General Information

- How many doctors and midwives attend births here? ____________
- On average, how many births per month occur here? ____________
- What's the ratio of patients to nurses during early labor? __________ Active labor? __________ Birth?__________ Postpartum?__________ Are these RNs or paraprofessionals, such as certified nursing assistants (CNAs) or licensed practical nurses (LPNs)?______________ Do you use floating nurses (nurses who work in many departments and may not have much experience in maternity nursing)?______________
- Do you encourage the use of birth plans? ______________

Labor Protocol

Birth Partners and Doulas

- Do you welcome doulas? ______________
- What's the birth partner's role? ______________
- Is my birth partner required to preregister?______________

- Does my birth partner need specific training courses? ____________
- May my birth partner film or photograph the labor, birth, and baby? ______
- Is more than one birth partner permitted? ____________
- What circumstances necessitate removal of a birth partner? ____________

____

Onset of Labor

Hospital Admission

- What entrance should I use during the day? ____________
  At night? ____________
- Who decides whether I should be admitted? ____________
- What is the admission criteria? ____________

  ____
- What is the admission procedure? ____________

  ____
  - Can I preregister? ____________
  - Where do I go to be admitted? ____________
  - What paperwork is required? ____________
- Does the time of admission affect my costs? ____________
- Do I incur any costs if I'm not admitted? ____________
- In the absence of my caregiver, who will attend my labor and delivery? ____________
- Will a birth plan signed by my caregiver be honored until my caregiver arrives? ____________
- What personal items may I bring? ____________

  ____

  ____

During Labor

- Will I be allowed to eat, drink, and use the bathroom during labor? ______

  ____
- How often are laboring women given intravenous (IV) fluids? ______

  ____
- What are your visitor policies during labor? ____________

  ____
- Will I be encouraged to walk during labor? ____________
- Under what circumstances will I be immobilized? ____________

  ____
- Does the site allow ____________? (Review birth plan.)

Vaginal Examinations

- How frequently are they administered during labor? ____________
- Who will administer the examinations? ____________

Monitoring Techniques

- What equipment is used to monitor the fetal heart rate during labor? ______

  ____

- How frequently are monitors used? ____________________
- Most frequently used form of monitoring ____________________
- Least frequently used form of monitoring ____________________

Specially Trained Personnel

- What types of skills are accessible? ____________________
- Availability of trained personnel ____________________

Comfort Measures

- Most frequently used comfort methods ____________________
- Are birth balls available? ____________________
- Does the site allow ____________________? (Review birth plan.)

Pain Relief

- What types of pain management are available? ____________________
- Is anesthesia available at all times? ____________________
- How frequently are medications administered? ____________________
- Most frequently used form of pain relief ____________________
- Least frequently used form of pain relief ____________________

Birth Protocol (Refer to your birth plan.)

Accommodations

- Does the facility allow labor and delivery in the same room (a birthing room)? ____________________
  - How many birthing rooms are available? ____________________
  - How frequently are they all occupied? ____________________
  - Can a birthing room be reserved? ____________________
  - What equipment is available in a birthing room? ____________________
  - If there are bathtubs, how often are they used for comforting a woman in labor? ____________ How many tubs do you have? ________ Do women ever give birth in the tubs? ____________________
- Does the facility have separate labor and delivery rooms? ____________
  - How many rooms of each type are available? ____________________
  - How frequently are they all occupied? ____________________
  - Can labor and delivery rooms be reserved? ____________________
  - What equipment is available in a labor room? ____________________

    ____

    In a delivery room? ____________________

Continuation of Care from Labor to Delivery

- Will the same monitors be used during labor and delivery? ____________
- Will the same pain management be used during labor and delivery? ________
- Will the same support staff attend during labor and delivery? ____________
- If no to any of the above, why not? ____________________

  ____

Episiotomy

- What is the staff's attitude toward episiotomies?____________________
- Will an effort be made to avoid an episiotomy? ____________________
- What pain management is available during and after an episiotomy? ____

____

Immediate Postpartum

- Will my birth partner be allowed to cut the cord?____________________
- Is cord blood harvesting available? ____________________
- How will the placenta be delivered? ____________________
- What will happen to the placenta? ____________________

Cesarean Section

- How many planned cesareans are scheduled per month?______________
- How many emergency cesareans are performed each month? __________
- If I have a planned cesarean, where will it take place? ______________
  How many people are allowed to attend? ____________________
  Who decides who can attend?____________________
- Where are emergency cesareans performed? ____________________
- What emergency facilities and staff are available for baby? __________

  ____

  Mother? ____
- What pain management is available during a cesarean?______________
- What pain management is available following a cesarean?____________

Recovery

- How long is the usual stay after a vaginal birth?______ Cesarean? ______
  May I stay longer?____________ Is there a set time for checkout?______
- What normally happens during postpartum recovery? ______________

  ____
- What are your visitor policies during postpartum? ________________

Baby Care Protocol (Refer to your birth plan.)

Immediate Care

- Where will the baby be placed immediately after birth?
  ◇Skin-to-skin with mother
  ◇On warming tray
- Does the facility use Apgar scoring? ____________________
- Can we hold the baby during the Apgar scoring? ________________
- Can my birth partner bathe the baby? ____________________
- Will I be able to nurse the baby within an hour after birth? __________
- Who takes responsibility for the baby during the immediate postpartum?

  ____

Neonatal Care

- Will the facility allow baby to room-in with mother? ________________
- For what reasons might baby be removed from mother's room? ____________

  ____

  How long might mother and baby be separated? ________________
- Who is allowed to transport baby through the facility? ______________

  How is baby transported? ________________________________

  May a parent accompany the baby when transported? ______________
- What procedures are routinely performed on newborns?
  - ◇Vitamin K injection
  - ◇Administration of an antibiotic ointment in the eyes
  - ◇Hearing screening
  - ◇Blood test for phenylketonuria (PKU)
  - ◇Blood test for hypothyroidism
  - ◇Blood test for galactosemia
  - ◇Blood test for sickle cell anemia and beta thalassemia
  - ◇Hepatitis B vaccination
- What level of care is available in the nursery? ____________________

  Will I have access to the nursery? ____________________________
- What is the procedure if medical problems arise? __________________

  ____
- What specialized staff is available?
  - ◇Pediatrician
  - ◇Neonatologist
  - ◇Respiratory therapist
  - ◇Social worker
  - ◇Development specialist
  - ◇Audiologist
  - ◇Other
- Will baby be transferred for specialized care?_____ If yes, to: __________

  ____
- What support staff is available for:
  - Basic childcare questions? ____________________________
  - Babies with special needs? ____________________________
- Do you have lactation consultants on staff?____ What are their working hours?

  ____

  May I call them after I go home if I have breastfeeding questions? _________

Administrative Protocol

Environment

- Cleanliness ____
- Security of:
  - Rooms ____
  - Nursery ____
  - Corridors ____

- How is public access limited? ______
- What procedures and policies are in place to prevent kidnapping? ______

______

- Rate of infections:
  - Maternal ______
  - Infant ______

Business Issues

- What are the estimated costs? ______
  - Will the facility provide a cost breakdown? ______
  - What additional charges might apply? ______

    ______

    ______

- Payment
  - Is the facility a participating provider for my insurance plan? ______
  - Will the facility bill me or my insurance company? ______
  - Is there a payment schedule? ______
  - Does the facility offer a sliding fee schedule? ______

Discharge

- What is the discharge procedure? ______
  - What paperwork is required? ______
  - Does discharge time affect costs? ______

Programs and Benefits

- Which of the following programs are available?
  - ◇Facility tours
  - ◇Nutrition classes
  - ◇Exercise classes or prenatal gym
  - ◇Birth classes
  - ◇Breastfeeding classes
  - ◇Sibling classes
  - ◇Photo of newborn
  - ◇Online nursery (website displaying newborn photos)
  - ◇Video of birth
  - ◇Phone-in service for questions about prenatal or newborn care
  - ◇Paperwork for birth certificate or social security card
  - ◇Visiting nurses
- Which of the following are provided free or at minimal cost to registered patients?
  - ◇Diapering supplies
  - ◇Baby feeding supplies
  - ◇Coupons from local merchants
  - ◇Literature

Home Birth

Choosing Home Birth

Ask yourself the following questions if you are considering giving birth to your baby at home. The more times you answer yes, the more appropriate home birth is for you.

- Are you having a healthy, low-risk pregnancy?
- Do you trust your body's natural ability to give birth?
- Is your primary motive for home birth a strong desire and commitment to birth at home? (Though home birth can save money, thrift should not be a primary or even secondary motive.)
- Are you secondarily motivated by a desire to avoid episiotomy, cesarean section, or epidural; a wish to be surrounded by loved ones; a desire for freedom to move around, change positions, take a shower, and eat freely during labor; and/or a yearning for the comforts of home and familiar surroundings?
- Are you willing to devote time and energy to finding the right birth attendant and assembling all the necessary gear, knowledge, and contacts?
- Do you feel comfortable taking charge of not only your birth experience, but also your health and your baby's health?
- Does your partner fully support your decision to give birth at home?
- Do you have a birth attendant who has attended many home births and is experienced and well informed in matters relevant to your circumstances?
- Do you have a fail-safe plan for transfer to a hospital, if necessary?

Preparing for Home Birth

Following is a list of recommendations collected from parents who've given birth at home and midwives who attend home births. Not all will be appropriate for your situation; skip those that don't make sense for you.

- Hire a midwife or physician to attend your baby's birth. Some tips on choosing a caregiver:
  - Ask about your caregiver's education, credentials, and experience attending home births.
  - Find out whether your caregiver has admitting privileges at a hospital or can at least accompany you and stay with you for labor support if you're transferred there.
  - If you choose a midwife, ensure that s/he has a working relationship with a physician. Find out who the consulting physician is and whether the physician is willing to take all home birth transfers.
  - Ask your caregiver what resuscitative equipment s/he would bring to your home, what complications s/he has encountered with newborns, and how s/he has handled them.

- Write a backup plan in case you need or want to be transferred to a hospital during labor.
- Find out what your backup hospital is like. (For example, is anesthesia available at all hours? Is there a neonatal intensive care unit? Do newborns usually room-in?)
- Pack an emergency hospital bag in case you need or want to transfer.
- Take a childbirth class.
- Write a birth plan and discuss it with your partner and your caregiver.
- As you approach your due date, find out what position your baby is in. (Occiput anterior—face-down—is ideal; breech is the least favorable position.) If necessary, discuss with your caregiver strategies for changing your baby's position.
- Read up on tricks to try if labor doesn't progress as you'd like, and let your birth partner know where to look for ideas on the big day.
- Think about comfort measures you may want during labor (for example, aromatherapy, massage, warm bath, music, hypnosis) and make sure the materials or people you'll need will be available.
- Stock up on some healthy, easy-to-digest food and drink for yourself, as well as some flexible straws and/or a sippy cup. Also, make sure there's food and drink available for your partner, caregiver, child(ren), or any others likely to be present.
- If your child(ren) will be present, arrange for supervision by an adult (besides you, your partner, or your caregiver). Brief this person on things to do or places to go if distraction becomes necessary or if you decide you're not comfortable with your child(ren) present.
- If you'll need any special birth gear that you don't already own, such as a birth pool, birth stool, or birth ball, rent or buy it.
- If you're planning a water birth, choose a birth pool site that won't be slippery when wet, and practice assembling and filling the pool.
- Wherever you plan to give birth, have clean towels; old sheets; and a plastic tarp, shower curtain, or tablecloth available.
- Have a hand-held mirror available in case you want to see the baby's head as it crowns.
- Do you want the baby to be born into a certain atmosphere (for example, with certain music playing or candles burning)? Tell your birth partner what you want.
- Have diapers, baby clothes, and blankets on hand.
- Make sure you have what you'll need for postpartum care, such as witch hazel pads and a cleansing bottle for a sore perineum.
- Choose a caregiver (for your child) who is supportive of your choice to give birth at home. Make arrangements for your baby to have a checkup twenty-four hours after birth.
- Find out the phone numbers of local lactation consultants in advance.
- Line up some postpartum household help.

Home Birth Gear Checklist

Here's a "shopping" list of items you may need for a home birth. Cross out those that don't apply to your situation and check off what remains as you gather up your gear.

Clothing

- ◇ Old or disposable underwear
- ◇ Old T-shirt or nightgown
- ◇ Baby clothes
- ◇ Diapers

Linens

- ◇ Receiving blankets
- ◇ Washcloths
- ◇ Towels
- ◇ Old sheets

Other Gear for Labor and Delivery

- ◇ Box of tissues
- ◇ Roll of cotton and scissors
- ◇ Hot compresses or hot-water bottles
- ◇ Acupressure wristbands for nausea
- ◇ Large pan and small bowl (for sterilizing, if necessary)
- ◇ Birth ball
- ◇ Birth stool
- ◇ Birth pool, bucket, hose long enough to reach faucet, and adaptor to fit your faucet
- ◇ Food and drink for you
- ◇ Food and drink for others
- ◇ Flexible straws or sippy cup
- ◇ Camera and film
- ◇ Stereo, CDs or tapes, and playlist
- ◇ Candles
- ◇ Hand-mirror
- ◇ Packed hospital bag in case of transfer (See page 220.)
- ◇ Plastic tarp, shower curtain, or tablecloth

Information

- ◇ Birth plan
- ◇ Reference books about childbirth
- ◇ Phone numbers of people to call after the birth
- ◇ Phone numbers of all caregivers, therapists, lactation consultants, and so on that may be needed during and after your baby's birth

Postpartum Supplies

- ◇ Sanitary pads
- ◇ Witch hazel pads
- ◇ Cleansing bottle
- ◇ Garbage bags
- ◇ Gift for older child(ren) from baby
- ◇ Celebratory food and drink
- ◇ Nice pajamas and robe to encourage resting for a few days (As one midwife says, a mom in pajamas or a robe is someone to be looked after. The same mom in jeans and a T-shirt is someone doing the looking after.)
- ◇ Notice for front door either inviting visitors in or politely sending them away
- ◇ A freezer full of prepared or easy-to-make meals
- ◇ Biological laundry detergent to remove stains from clothing and linens
- ◇ Hydrogen peroxide to remove bloodstains from carpets if necessary

Prenatal Checkups

Tracking your prenatal checkups can be very interesting. Your body is changing rapidly, and your baby's development is fascinating to observe. Information recorded at your checkups can be very useful in subsequent pregnancies, especially if you change caregivers.

Initially, your caregiver will ask you for a medical history. It's helpful to go over this information ahead of time, to save time and head-scratching at your caregiver's office. Be sure to review your medical history with your partner, especially if your partner won't be attending the first prenatal checkup.

As your pregnancy progresses, you can record both clinical and personal observations about you and your baby.

Medical History Organizer

Mother's Medical History

List any allergies you have. ______________________________

____

____

List any medications, vitamins, and/or herbs you're currently taking. ______

____

____

____

Note any of the following conditions you've had:

- ◇ Alcohol or drug addiction
- ◇ Anemia or blood disorder
- ◇ Anesthetic complication
- ◇ Asthma
- ◇ Back problem
- ◇ Birth defect
- ◇ Blood clots
- ◇ Bone disease
- ◇ Cancer
- ◇ Chickenpox
- ◇ Chromosomal abnormalities
- ◇ Depression or anxiety
- ◇ Diabetes
- ◇ Eating disorder
- ◇ Epilepsy or seizures
- ◇ Gastrointestinal problem
- ◇ Genetic disease (Tay-Sachs disease, sickle cell anemia, cystic fibrosis, phenylketonuria [PKU])
- ◇ Heart problem
- ◇ Hepatitis
- ◇ Hypertension
- ◇ Immune disorder
- ◇ Jaundice
- ◇ Joint problem
- ◇ Kidney problem
- ◇ Measles, mumps, or rubella
- ◇ Mental illness
- ◇ Migraines
- ◇ Muscle disease
- ◇ Neurological disorder
- ◇ Respiratory problem

- Tetanus
- Thyroid disorder
- Tuberculosis
- Urinary problem
- Vascular problem

Note any of the following procedures you've had:

- Chromosome test
- Blood transfusion
- Vaccination
- Infertility test
- Surgery

Mother's Gynecological History

Date of first day of last period ______________________

Age at menarche (first period) ______________________

Frequency of periods ______________________

Duration of periods ______________________

Amount of bleeding between periods (none, spotting, light, heavy) __________

Premenstrual symptoms ______________________

Menopausal symptoms ______________________

Last Pap smear ______________________

Result ______________________

Number of abnormal Pap smears ______________________

Treatment ______________________

Most recent method of contraception ______________________

History of gynecological problems (endometriosis, fibroid tumor, ovarian cyst, cancer, diethylstilbestrol [DES] exposure, infertility, sexually transmitted disease, other) ______________________

____

____

____

Mother's Obstetrical History

In the chart below, note the pertinent details of any pregnancies you've had before this one. Use one column for each pregnancy.

Pregnancy	1	2	3	4	5
Approximate conception date					
Miscarriage (week of pregnancy)					
Abortion					
Stillbirth					
Live birth (week of pregnancy)					

Mother's Obstetrical History (continued)

Pregnancy	1	2	3	4	5
Number of babies					
Length of labor					
Vaginal delivery					
Pain medication used					
Cesarean section (planned or emergency)					
Preeclampsia					
Fetal distress					
Prolonged labor (over 30 hours)					
Other problems (specify)					
Difficult delivery (explain)					

Family Medical History

Note whether the baby's father or a blood relative of either of you has had any of the following conditions.

- ◇ Anemia or blood disorder
- ◇ Asthma
- ◇ Birth defect
- ◇ Blood clots
- ◇ Bone disease
- ◇ Cancer
- ◇ Chromosomal abnormalities
- ◇ DES exposure
- ◇ Diabetes
- ◇ Endometriosis
- ◇ Epilepsy or seizures
- ◇ Fibroid tumor
- ◇ Gastrointestinal problem
- ◇ Genetic disease (Tay-Sachs disease, sickle cell anemia, cystic fibrosis, PKU)
- ◇ Heart problem
- ◇ Hepatitis
- ◇ Hypertension
- ◇ Immune disorder
- ◇ Jaundice
- ◇ Kidney problem
- ◇ Mental illness
- ◇ Mental retardation
- ◇ Multiple births
- ◇ Muscle disease
- ◇ Neural tube defect (spina bifida, meningocele, anencephaly)
- ◇ Neurological disorder
- ◇ Respiratory problem
- ◇ Miscarriage
- ◇ Stillbirth
- ◇ Thyroid disorder
- ◇ Vascular problem

Possible High-Risk Factors

In addition to analyzing your medical history, your caregiver might ask about the following possible high-risk factors:

- Are you over age thirty-four or under age sixteen?
- Have you had any vaginal bleeding?
- Are you overweight or underweight?
- Have you been exposed to chemicals and/or radiation?
- Do you smoke cigarettes?
- Do you drink alcohol and/or take illegal substances?
- Is your daily caffeine intake excessive (more than 300 milligrams)?
- Do you exercise infrequently (less than twice a week)?
- Are you in an abusive relationship?
- Are either you or the baby's father of Jewish, French Canadian, African American, or Mediterranean ancestry? (These ancestries have higher incidences of certain congenital conditions.)
- What is your blood type, including Rh factor? What is the baby's father's?
- Have you had a previous injection of Rho(D) immunoglobulin?

Symptoms of Pregnancy

Your caregiver may want to note whether you're experiencing any of the following symptoms.

Symptom	When Experienced
Nausea	
Vomiting	
Fatigue	
Headache	
Visual problems	
Edema (fluid retention)	
Urinary problems	
Constipation	
Bleeding	
Anemia	
Other:	

Obstetrical Record and Calendar

The form that follows will help you record the progress of your pregnancy at each prenatal checkup. In the the column labeled "Fundus," record the measurement from the top of your uterus to your pelvic bone.

Week	Date	Weight	Blood Pressure	Pulse	Fundus	Baby's Heart Rate

Week-to-Week Observations

Note: All pregnancies are different. The timing of maternal changes and fetal development isn't exact, and not all women experience all symptoms.

Week	Maternal Changes	Fetal Development	Questions/ Comments
	First Trimester		
1–4	Missed menstrual period; light spotting possible	0.014 to 0.04 inches long; cells already specialized according to functions	
5	May experience nausea, tingling or sore breasts, and darkened areolas; frequent urination; fatigue	0.05 inches long; heart, brain, spinal cord, muscles, and bones developing	
6	Slight weight gain possible in waist, legs, and breasts; may experience heartburn, constipation, and food cravings	0.08 to 0.16 inches crown to rump; brain, eyes, and limb buds forming; heart contractions begin	
7	More aware of body changes; may still experience nausea, tingly and tender breasts, and other symptoms of early pregnancy	0.44 to 0.52 inches crown to rump; hands and feet have digital plates where fingers and toes will develop; eyes, nostrils, intestines, heart, and lungs becoming more developed; brain and spinal cord growing from neural tube	
8	Uterus grows to size of grapefruit; may feel cramping or pain in lower abdomen or sides	0.56 to 0.8 inches crown to rump; eyelid folds and ears forming; tip of nose visible	
9	Uterus continuing to grow; waistline thickening; weight gain possibly still slight due to food aversions, cravings, heartburn, indigestion, nausea, and bloating; mood swings and weepiness common	0.9 to 1.2 inches crown to rump; arms and legs longer; head more erect and neck more developed; moves body and limbs, visible by ultrasound but not felt	

Week	Maternal Changes	Fetal Development	Questions/ Comments
10	May continue to feel tired and moody; may wear looser clothes	1.25 to 1.68 inches crown to rump; most physical malformations, if any, have occurred by this time; eyes covered by skin that will eventually split	
11	Uterus almost big enough to fill pelvis and may be felt in lower abdomen; may experience changes in hair, skin, or nail growth	1.75 to 2.4 inches crown to rump; weighs about 0.3 ounce; fingernails appear; external genitalia showing distinguishing characteristics; is swallowing and kicking but still not felt	
12	Nausea starts to fade; energy starts to return; may experience occasional headaches, dizziness, and fatigue; 3 to 5 pounds gained overall	2.5 inches crown to rump; weighs 0.3 to 0.5 ounce; body fully formed, from tooth buds to toenails	
13	Uterus filling pelvis and starting to grow upward into abdomen; stretch marks may appear on breasts and abdomen; breasts enlarging	2.6 to 3.1 inches crown to rump; weighs 0.5 to 0.7 ounce; eyes moving closer together; toes and fingers clearly separate; ankles and wrists formed; intestines shifting into place	
14	Skin and muscles starting to stretch; may have some constipation	3.2 to 4.1 inches crown to rump; weighs about 1 ounce; ears shifting from neck to sides of head; neck lengthening and chin becoming prominent; facial features and fingerprints formed; beginning to respond to outside stimuli	

Week	Maternal Changes	Fetal Development	Questions/ Comments
	Second Trimester		
15	Can feel uterus about 3 to 4 inches below navel	4.1 to 4.5 inches crown to rump; weighs about 1.75 ounces; body covered with downy hair (lanugo); eyebrows beginning to grow; may suck thumb; bones hardening	
16	Uterus about 3 inches below navel and weighs about 8.75 ounces; may begin to feel baby's movements; may have nosebleeds; veins may become more visible; frequency of urination may decrease	4.3 to 4.6 inches crown to rump; weighs about 2.8 ounces; nervous system functioning and muscles responding to stimulation from brain; heartbeat audible with Doptone (hand-held ultrasound tool)	
17	Obvious swelling in lower abdomen; 5 to 10 pounds gained overall; may have increased appetite	4.4 to 4.8 inches crown to rump; weighs about 3.5 ounces; fat begins to form, helping heat production and metabolism; circulatory and urinary systems functioning; hair on head, eyebrows, and eyelashes growing	
18	Uterus about size of cantaloupe and felt just below navel; can feel baby move; heart works 40 to 50 percent harder to support pregnancy	5 to 5.6 inches crown to rump; weighs about 5.25 ounces; can yawn, stretch, hiccup, frown; taste buds developing; retinas sensitive to light	
19	May feel lower abdominal aches, dizziness, heartburn, constipation, leg cramps, mild swelling of ankles and feet, and backache; may develop tiny, temporary red marks (spider nevi) on face, shoulders, and arms	5.2 to 6 inches crown to rump; weighs about 7 ounces; skin developing; protective coating (vernix) developing	

Week	Maternal Changes	Fetal Development	Questions/ Comments
20	Uterus even with navel; risk of urinary tract infections increases; breathing becomes deeper; may perspire more	5.6 to 6.4 inches crown to rump; weighs about 9 ounces; can hear sounds; moves often	
21	Uterus starting to extend above navel; 10 to 14 pounds gained overall	7.2 inches crown to rump; weighs about 10.5 ounces; organ systems maturing; buds for permanent teeth forming	
22	May still have leg and foot cramps, mild swelling of ankles and feet	7.6 inches crown to rump; weighs about 12.25 ounces; muscles strengthening; eyelids and eyebrows developed	
23	Round belly pronounced; 12 to 15 pounds gained overall; vaginal secretions increase; may still have backaches	8 inches crown to rump; weighs about 1 pound; body becoming proportioned; wrinkled skin; lanugo may darken	
24	Uterus 1.5 to 2 inches above navel; weight gain now about a pound per week	8.4 inches crown to rump; weighs about 1.2 pounds; starting to produce white blood cells	
25	Uterus may be expanding into sides of abdomen; may experience hemorrhoids	8.8 inches crown to rump; weighs about 1.5 pounds; skin opaque; heartbeat can be heard through stethoscope or by putting ear against belly	
26	May feel rib pain, indigestion, heartburn, and pains down sides of abdomen	9.2 inches crown to rump; weighs almost 2 pounds; hearing fully developed; lungs still growing; has sleeping and waking patterns	
27	May develop stretch marks; 16 to 22 pounds gained overall; balance and mobility may change	9.6 inches crown to rump; weighs a little more than 2 pounds; hands active; can get thumb into mouth; can cry	

Week	Maternal Changes	Fetal Development	Questions/ Comments
	Third Trimester		
28	Uterus extends well above navel; may experience leg cramps and mildly swollen ankles and feet; insomnia; shortness of breath; lower abdominal aches; clumsiness; scattered Braxton-Hicks contractions; frequent urination	10 inches crown to rump; weighs about 2.4 pounds; eyelids opening; branches of lungs developing; brain tissue increasing	
29	Uterus 3.5 to 4 inches above navel; 19 to 25 pounds gained overall	10.4 inches crown to rump; weighs about 2.7 pounds; kicks and stretches but becoming more confined	
30	Uterus 4 inches above navel; may feel pelvic and abdominal discomfort	17 inches head to toe; weighs about 3 pounds; growing plumper; eyebrows and eyelashes fully developed; hair on head thickening; head and body proportioned; hands fully formed and fingernails growing	
31	Uterus now fills large part of abdomen; 21 to 27 pounds gained overall	18 inches head to toe; weighs about 3.5 pounds; nerve endings in ears connected	
32	May continue to have backaches and leg cramps; may also notice colostrum leaking from breasts	18.9 inches head to toe; weighs almost 4 pounds; fills almost all space in uterus; layer of fat forming underneath skin; practices opening eyes and breathing	
33	Uterus about 5.2 inches above navel; 22 to 28 pounds gained overall; may experience persistent heartburn	19.4 inches head to toe; weighs about 4.4 pounds; begins to move less now; body curls up with knees bent, chin resting on chest, and arms and legs crossed	

Week	Maternal Changes	Fetal Development	Questions/ Comments
34	Uterus pushing against lower ribs; Braxton-Hicks contractions may increase; pelvis expands and may ache or feel tingly; navel probably pushing out	19.8 inches head to toe; weighs almost 5 pounds; organs almost fully mature, except for lungs; fingernails reach ends of fingers, but toenails not yet fully grown; movements less frequent	
35	Uterus about 6 inches above navel; 24 to 29 pounds gained overall; may have trouble getting comfortable and sleeping	20.25 inches head to toe; weighs little more than 5.5 pounds; lungs almost fully developed; still not enough fat deposits beneath skin to keep warm outside womb	
36	Uterus probably up under ribs; may alternate between feeling tired and energetic; may experience increased backache and heaviness, constipation, heartburn, and discomfort in buttocks and pelvis	20.7 inches head to toe; weighs about 6 pounds; may drop lower in abdomen, usually turning head down; brain developing rapidly	
37	Uterus may not have grown; 25 to 35 pounds gained overall	21 inches head to toe; weighs about 6.5 pounds; growing rounder; skin getting pinker and less wrinkly; head usually positioned down into pelvis	
38	Probably not growing bigger, but may feel more uncomfortable	21 inches head to toe; weighs about 6.8 pounds; most of lanugo and vernix disappearing; getting antibodies from mother; overall growth slowing, but fat cells under skin growing plumper	

Week	Maternal Changes	Fetal Development	Questions/ Comments
39	Uterus has filled pelvis and most of abdomen; may feel large and uncomfortable; center of gravity has shifted, causing clumsiness	21.5 inches head to toe; weighs little more than 7 pounds; toenails and fingernails grown to tips of toes and fingers; muscles of arms and legs strong; practicing lung movements; head drops into pelvis if head down	
40	More difficult to find comfortable position to sleep	21.5 inches from head to toe; weighs about 7.5 pounds; reflexes coordinated so baby can blink, close eyes, turn head, grasp firmly and respond to sounds, light, and touch; more lanugo falls out, but some may remain at birth on shoulders, folds of skin, and backs of ears	

Nutrition

A balanced diet during pregnancy is essential for both you and your developing baby. The foods you eat must support not only your energy requirements, but also the additional demands of your increased blood volume, breast development, fetus, placenta, and membranes.

Average Pregnancy Weight Gain

If your prepregnancy weight was normal for your height, you should gain twenty-five to thirty-five pounds. If your prepregnancy weight was below normal, you should gain twenty-eight to forty pounds. If your prepregnancy weight was above normal, you should gain fifteen to twenty-five pounds. The average distribution of pregnancy weight is as follows:

Pounds	Tissue
4–14 pounds	Fat stores
8½ pounds	Increased blood and fluids
1–2 pounds	Breasts
2 pounds	Enlarged uterus
7½ pounds	Baby
1½ pounds	Placenta

Weight gain varies. Generally, you should gain two to four pounds during the first trimester and close to one pound per week during the second and third trimesters.

Plotting Your Pregnancy Weight Gain

Each week follow these steps to monitor your pregnancy weight gain.

Step 1: Subtract your prepregnancy weight from your current weight. The difference is the number of pounds you've gained.

Step 2: Find that number on the vertical axis.

Step 3: Find the week of your pregnancy on the horizontal axis.

Step 4: Mark the point on the graph where the line corresponding to the pounds you've gained intersects with the line corresponding to your pregnancy week.

Step 5: Draw a line from last week's dot to this week's dot.

Your Pregnancy Weight Gain

Your Changing Shape

A visual record of your changing shape is fun to see. In the first box on the next page, attach a photo of your prepregnant self. When you're close to your due date, have someone take a photo of you, then attach it, too. You'll be amazed at the difference!

Prepregnancy Photo

Date taken:

Full-Term Photo

Date taken:

Daily Food Needs

Food Group	Daily Servings	Sample Servings	Notes
Grains	8 or more	1 slice bread; ½ small bagel; ½ cup cooked rice, pasta, cereal, bulgur, barley, or quinoa; 1 ounce ready-to-eat cereal, 3–4 crackers	Whole grains should make up 3 or more servings.
Fruits	4 or more	1 medium fresh fruit; ½ grapefruit, mango, or papaya; ¼ cup dried fruit; ½ cup canned or cut fruit; ¾ cup fruit juice	Eat at least one fruit or vegetable that's high in vitamin C and one that's orange or dark green every day.
Vegetables	4 or more	½ cup cooked vegetables, 1 cup leafy vegetables, 1 small potato, ¾ cup vegetable juice	Eat at least one fruit or vegetable that's high in vitamin C and one that's orange or dark green every day.
Calcium-rich foods	4 or more	1 cup dairy milk or yogurt, 1 cup calcium-fortified orange juice or soymilk, 1½ ounces natural cheese, 2 ounces processed cheese	
Protein foods	3	2–3 ounces cooked lean meat; 2 eggs; ½ cup tuna; ½ cup legumes, tofu, or textured vegetable protein (TVP); 2 tablespoons nuts or nut butter	Eat fish at least once a week. (Consult your caregiver, call 888-SAFEFOOD, or visit http://www.foodsafety.gov for guidelines on safe fish consumption.) Eat an additional ½ protein serving for each of your 4 servings of calcium-rich foods that isn't a dairy product.
Fats and sweets	Eat sparingly.	Most fat and sugar is hidden in foods from the groups listed above.	Fats should comprise no more than 30 percent of calories consumed daily.

Food Guide Pyramid for Pregnancy

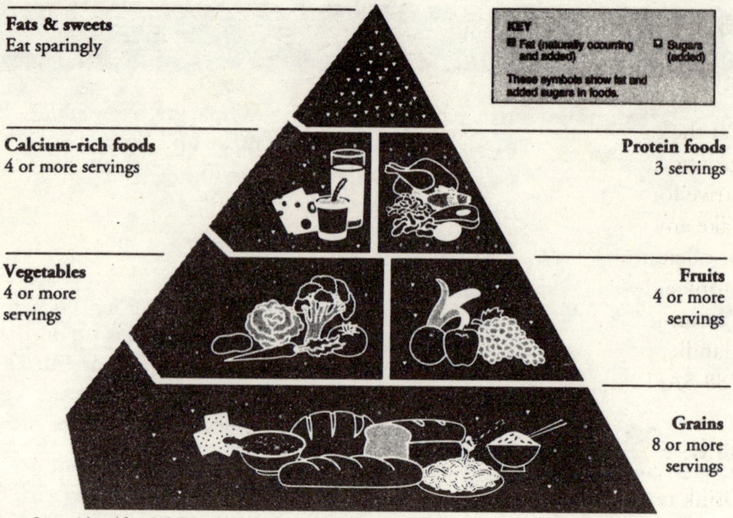

Source: Adapted from U.S. Department of Agriculture/U.S. Department of Health and Human Services Food Guide Pyramid.

Diet Diary

Write down in the following spaces everything you've eaten during the last day (or on a typical day). Then refer to Daily Food Needs on page 43 to tally the number of servings of each food type you've eaten.

Meal	Foods and Drinks
Breakfast	
Snack	
Lunch	
Snack	
Dinner	
Snack	

Compare your totals for the day with those recommended. If necessary, use this information to consult with your caregiver.

Dietary Dos and Don'ts

Do:

- Eat the recommended number of servings from each of the five main food groups. (See page 43.)
- Strive for variety in your diet.
- Take any supplemental vitamins or minerals (especially folic acid, iron, or calcium) recommended by your caregiver.
- Drink at least eight glasses of water daily.
- Consume salt in moderation.
- Handle, cook, and store food safely to prevent food-borne illness. (Call 888-SAFEFOOD or visit http://www.foodsafety.gov for more information.)

Don't:

- Drink unpasteurized milk.
- Eat unpasteurized cheeses or any kind of pâté.
- Eat liver products.
- Eat highly processed foods.
- Eat large amounts of fat or sugar.
- Eat or drink large amounts of caffeine.
- Drink alcohol.
- Eat shark, swordfish, tuna steaks, sea bass, or other fish that may contain high levels of mercury. (Consult your caregiver, call 888-SAFEFOOD, or visit http://www.foodsafety.gov for guidelines on safe fish consumption.)
- Consume herbs or herbal teas without your caregiver's approval.

Common Discomforts

You may have a hard time mustering the energy or enthusiasm to get organized for your baby if pregnancy symptoms are hitting you hard. The next few pages will help you manage three of the most common pregnancy discomforts: constipation, nausea, and fatigue.

Constipation

A slowing digestive system, pressure from a growing baby, and iron supplements cause constipation in many pregnant women. If you're suffering from constipation, try the following suggestions with your caregiver's approval.

Constipation Remedies

Remedy	Helped	Didn't Help
Exercise regularly.		
Drink plenty of fluids.		
Eat high-fiber foods such as fruits, vegetables, whole grains, bran, and prune juice.		
Avoid foods that tend to constipate you, such as meat, cheese, or bananas.		
Avoid caffeine.		
Try an over-the-counter product containing psyllium husk.		
If you're taking an iron supplement, ask your caregiver to recommend one that's less constipating.		
Go to the bathroom as soon as you feel the urge to have a bowel movement.		
Eat 1 or 2 tablespoons of molasses per day (in milk, warm water, or cereal or over pancakes).		
Add 2 tablespoons of ground raw flaxseed to water, juice, tea, or cereal.		

Pregnancy Nausea

Unlike the misnomer *morning sickness* suggests, pregnancy nausea can occur any time of the day or night, and can be triggered by almost anything. Following are some of the most common culprits. Once you identify a trigger, the pregnancy nausea survival kit and suggested remedies on pages 48–50 may help alleviate your symptoms.

Pregnancy Nausea Triggers

Trigger	Problem	No Problem
Eating and Drinking		
Undereating (empty stomach)		
Overeating		
Dehydration		
Spicy foods		
Fatty foods		
Gassy foods		
Vitamin and mineral supplements		
Medications and herbs		

Trigger	Problem	No Problem
Odors		
Food odors		
Perfumes		
Body odors		
Scented products		
Gasoline and exhaust		
Cleaning products		
Paint		
Cigarette smoke		
Pet odors		
Coffee		
Garbage		
Activity, Motion, or Position		
Sudden change of position		
Riding in vehicle		
Vigorous activity		
Lying flat on back		
Fatigue		
Sights		
Bright lights		
Glare		
Leftover food		
Sounds		
Loud noises		
Sudden noises		
Fast or loud music		
Traffic		
Sirens		
Construction sites		
Emotions		
Stress		
Strong emotions		
Monotony or boredom		

Trigger	Problem	No Problem
Touch and Temperature		
Tight clothing (especially around abdomen, waist, or neck)		
Brushing teeth		
Poor ventilation		
Drastic temperature change		
Hot weather		
Cold weather		
Humidity		

Pregnancy Nausea Survival Kit

Carry the following items with you at all times:

Item	Comments
High-protein/ high-carbohydrate snacks	Snacks like peanuts, soda crackers, and granola bars help soak up excess stomach acid and prevent blood sugar swings that can lead to nausea.
Hard candy	Sucking on something tart or sweet sometimes helps ease nausea.
Unscented moist towelettes	Use to refresh your face after a bout of nausea or vomiting.
Travel-size toothbrush, toothpaste, and chewing gum or breath mints	Use to clean your mouth and freshen your breath after vomiting.
Fan	Fanning yourself sometimes helps if you feel suffocated by still air.
Acupressure wristbands	If these little accessories (often used for motion sickness) work for you, you'll want to keep them on hand.
Small plastic bag	Use as a barf bag. (It can also hold the kit items.)

Pregnancy Nausea Remedies

Suggestion	Helped	Didn't Help
Food and Drink		
Eat small, frequent meals to avoid having an empty or too-full stomach.		
Eat more healthy proteins and complex carbohydrates.		
Eat a snack before getting out of bed.		
Eat a snack before going to bed.		
Increase foods rich in vitamin B_6 or take vitamin B_6 supplements. (Check with your caregiver first.)		
Take ginger supplements, suck on a piece of peeled ginger root, or drink natural ginger ale. (Check with your caregiver first.)		
Avoid foods that trigger nausea, such as fatty or gassy foods.		
Eat or drink whatever sounds good (choosing healthy options when possible).		
Identify foods and beverages that alleviate nausea. Do they have tastes or textures in common? (For example, are they salty, bitter, tart, soft, crunchy, bland, or spicy?) If so, try other foods in the same category.		
Take vitamins with your biggest meal of the day.		
Drink liquids throughout the day to avoid dehydration.		
Drink liquids between, not with, meals and snacks.		
Avoid caffeinated beverages.		
Drink decaffeinated herbal teas. (Consult your caregiver about which teas are safe.)		
Drink liquids that are hot or cold.		
Drink acidic juices on a full stomach. (Try lemonade.)		
Drink carbonated beverages.		

Suggestion	Helped	Didn't Help
Daily Routine		
If you don't have to wake up at a set time, don't. Get as much rest as possible and ease into your day.		
Keep a damp cloth at your bedside and place over your eyes or on your forehead when you feel nauseated.		
Carry unscented moist towelettes during the day.		
Change positions slowly, especially upon awakening in the morning.		
Avoid strong odors and/or any other nausea triggers.		
Exercise.		
Get fresh air.		
Get out and do something you enjoy. A pleasant activity or change of scenery may distract you from your nausea and provide some relief.		
When traveling by car, be a driver instead of a passenger.		
Undergo acupressure treatments or wear acupressure wristbands.		
Reduce stress.		
Wear loose clothing.		
With your caregiver's approval, try a chewable antacid.		
Consult with your caregiver about prescription drugs that may relieve nausea symptoms.		
Try to think positive and keep your eyes on the prize: your baby!		

Fatigue

Fatigue is common during the first and last trimesters of pregnancy. However, proper rest is essential throughout the entire forty weeks. Because your body requires more rest, consider some of the strategies offered in this section.

Strategies for Reducing Fatigue

Napping

- Nap whenever you can throughout the day.
- If you're an at-home mom, nap while your child naps, plays at a friend's house, or attends school or playgroup.
- If you work outside the home, nap during breaks. Set an alarm so you don't oversleep. If your own workspace isn't quiet, nap in a lounge, empty office, or even a storage room—anyplace that's quiet, safe, and comfortable.

Sleeping at Night

- Go to bed as early as possible.
- Sleep in as late as possible.
- Make yourself as comfortable as possible at night to help you sleep well. If necessary, sleep alone, use extra pillows, add or subtract a blanket, or sleep on a couch or recliner—whatever works for you.
- Ask your partner to tend to a child who doesn't sleep through the night so your sleep won't be interrupted.

Eating and Drinking

- Eat a nutritious meal or snack at least every two to three hours.
- Drink water throughout the day.
- If recommended by your caregiver, take vitamin supplements to fill any gaps in your diet.

Prioritizing

- Limit nonessential activities (including housework) that prevent you from getting adequate rest.
- Get fresh air and exercise regularly, which will both rejuvenate you during the day and help you sleep better at night.

Adjusting Your Work Schedule

- Take a vacation day or sick day (or half-day) in the middle of the week every now and then.
- Negotiate a flexible work schedule with your boss so you can rest when you're feeling low and work efficiently when you're feeling well. For example, you might work at home sometimes or go to the office in the evening or on the weekend to catch up.
- Negotiate a job-share with a coworker.
- Work part-time instead of full-time.

Environmental Hazards

Whether an environmental hazard affects a pregnant woman or her baby depends on the quantity, timing, duration, and manner of exposure. Use the following checklist to assess your exposure to environmental hazards and reduce it, if necessary.

You Might Be Exposed If...	To Reduce Your Exposure...
Hazard: lead **Risks:** miscarriage, preterm delivery, low birth weight, developmental delays, learning and behavioral problems	
• Your home was built when lead paint was common (before 1978). • Your home has lead pipes, lead solder on copper pipes, or brass faucets. • You use lead crystal glassware or handcrafted ceramic dishes frequently. • You use scented candles, hand tools with plastic grips, oil paints, ceramic glazes, or stained glass materials frequently. • Anyone in your household is a painter or construction worker or works at a smelter, auto repair shop, or battery manufacturing plant. • You use a hair dye that contains lead acetate.	• Don't remove lead-based paint if it isn't crumbling or peeling. • To remove lead-based paint, hire a professional and stay away until the project is done. • Ask your state health department how to get your pipes tested. • Run tap water for thirty seconds before using it for drinking or cooking. Use cold water only. • Use a water filter that removes lead. Change as recommended. • Don't use lead crystal glassware or handcrafted ceramics. • Don't use scented candles, hand tools with plastic grips, oil paints, ceramic glazes, or stained glass materials. • Workers exposed to lead should change and shower at work. Wash contaminated clothes at work or separately at home. • Never use hair dyes that contain lead acetate.

You Might Be Exposed If...	To Reduce Your Exposure...
Hazard: arsenic **Risks:** miscarriage, stillbirth	
• You live near a metal smelter, hazardous waste site, or incinerator or in an area where arsenic fertilizers were used. • Anyone in your household works in metal smelting, semiconductor manufacturing, or herbicide application. • You're using treated lumber for a home construction project.	• Drink bottled water or ask your state health department how to get your water tested. • Limit your contact with soil. • Workers exposed to arsenic should change and shower at work. Wash contaminated clothes at work or separately at home. • Stay away from home construction projects.
Hazard: cadmium **Risks:** damage to placenta, low birth weight	
• Anyone in your household works in semiconductor manufacturing, welding, soldering, ceramics, or painting. • You use fungicides, fabric dyes, ceramic and glass glazes, or fertilizers that contain cadmium.	• Workers exposed to cadmium should change and shower at work. Wash contaminated clothes at work or separately at home. • Don't use products that contain cadmium.
Hazard: pesticides **Risks:** miscarriage, preterm delivery, birth defects	
• You eat conventionally grown fruits and vegetables. • You use pesticides in your home or on your property.	• Eat organic fruits and vegetables. • Wash all fruits and vegetables with soap and water before eating them. • Use less-toxic pesticides like boric acid. • When toxic pesticides are applied indoors: ~ Remove food, dishes, and utensils from the treatment area. ~ Have someone else apply the pesticide. ~ Stay away from the treated area as long as the manufacturer recommends. ~ Afterward, have someone else open the windows and wash all food preparation surfaces.

You Might Be Exposed If…	To Reduce Your Exposure…
	• When toxic pesticides are applied outdoors: ~ Close all windows and turn off air conditioning. ~ Wear rubber gloves when gardening.
Hazard: deet (diethyl toluamide) **Risk:** inadequate proof of safety during pregnancy	
• You frequently use insect repellents.	• Use deet-free insect repellents. • If you must use deet-based repellent, apply it sparingly to your clothes, not your skin.
Hazard: organic solvents **Risks:** miscarriage, birth defects	
• You work in a semiconductor plant or your work involves photography, dye, or silk-screen printing. • You use alcohols, degreasers, paint thinners, varnish removers, or lacquers for arts and crafts projects. • You use household cleaning products that contain organic solvents.	• Make sure your work area is well ventilated and wear appropriate protective equipment, including gloves and a facemask. • Use nontoxic commercial or homemade cleaning products. • Never eat or drink in your work area. • Ask your employer for the Material Safety Data Sheets (MSDSs) for the products you use or visit http://www.cdc.gov/niosh/topics/chemical-safety to find online MSDS resources.
Hazard: chlorination byproducts **Risks:** miscarriage, birth defects, poor fetal growth	
• Your tap water is chlorinated.	• Install a carbon filter on your kitchen faucet and showerhead. Drink, cook, and shower with filtered water. • Take shorter showers and baths. • Drink unchlorinated bottled water.

You Might Be Exposed If…	To Reduce Your Exposure…
	• Call the Environmental Protection Agency's (EPA's) safe-water hotline (800-426-4791) for the latest information on water quality.
Hazard: household cleaning products **Risks:** miscarriage, birth defects, death	
• You use cleaning products that contain organic solvents. • You use cleaning products that contain ammonia or chlorine.	• Make sure your work area is well ventilated. • Wear gloves. • Never eat or drink in your work area. • Never mix products containing ammonia and chlorine. The chemical reaction produces deadly chlorine gas and/or explosion. • Use nontoxic commercial or homemade cleaning products. For shopping tips and recipes, visit http://www.environmentalhealth.org/fs-homeclean.html.
Hazard: secondhand smoke **Risk:** low birth weight	
• Someone smokes regularly in your home or workplace. • You regularly visit homes or businesses in which people smoke.	• Don't permit others to smoke in your home. • If someone insists on smoking in your home, open windows or use exhaust fans to improve ventilation. • If your workplace doesn't control secondhand smoke effectively, work with management and your labor organization (if applicable) to establish one. • Don't visit homes where people smoke. • Patronize only businesses that are smoke-free or have well-ventilated nonsmoking areas. Ask to be seated in nonsmoking areas as far as possible from smokers.

You Might Be Exposed If…	To Reduce Your Exposure…
Hazard: hair dyes, bleaches, permanents, and relaxers **Risk:** inadequate proof of safety during pregnancy	
• You regularly dye, bleach, perm, or straighten your hair. • You use a hair dye that contains lead acetate.	• Avoid hair treatments during your pregnancy or at least during the first trimester. • Use a vegetable dye like henna. Check the product label to make sure the dye doesn't contain toxic chemicals. • Instead of dyeing your hair, highlight, paint, or frost it to expose fewer chemicals to your scalp. • Never use hair dyes that contain lead acetate.
Hazard: x-rays **Risks:** birth defects, cancer, miscarriage	
• You work with or near radiation (for example, in a hospital radiography lab or a food irradiation facility). • You receive frequent medical or dental x-rays.	• Find out your employer's radiation protection policy for pregnant employees. Discuss temporary reassignment or other appropriate arrangements. • Avoid having medical and dental x-rays while pregnant, or have only absolutely necessary ones. Tell your caregiver or technician that you're pregnant, and wear a lead apron.
Hazard: viruses and parasites **Risks:** fetal infection, miscarriage, birth defects, physical and mental delays	
• You work at a hospital, emergency service, prison, childcare center, school, or other facility that may harbor viruses like hepatitis B, human immunodeficiency virus (HIV), herpes, or rubella. • You work with animals or soil or change the litter box of a pet cat, any of which may harbor the toxoplasma parasite.	• Wear protective clothing, including gloves and a facemask, when handling blood products, soil, or animal waste. • Discuss with your employer ways to reduce your exposure to infectious hazards, such as temporary reassignment. • Have someone else change the litter box of a pet cat.

Prenatal Classes

Some families enjoy taking classes during pregnancy. Exercise sessions and educational programs help you get your mind and body in shape for pregnancy, childbirth, and parenthood. Use the following pages to help you investigate and choose from the options available to you.

Types of Classes

Here's a list of typical birth and family classes offered in many communities.

Educational

- Prenatal nutrition
- Childbirth preparation (usually for first-time parents)
- Childbirth refresher (for veteran parents)
- Cesarean preparation
- VBAC (vaginal birth after cesarean) preparation
- Special situations (teen pregnancy, high-risk pregnancy, same-sex parents, pregnancy after a loss, bed rest, baby with special needs, premature baby, multiples)
- Sibling preparation
- Children at birth
- Breastfeeding
- Baby care
- Infant and child first aid and cardiopulmonary resuscitation (CPR)
- Fatherhood
- Parenting
- Grandparenting
- Preparation for religious ceremony after the birth
- Mom and baby support group
- Returning to work

Physical

- Pregnancy exercise (low-impact aerobics, water exercise, yoga)
- Organized activities for expectant parents (lap swimming, walking, biking)
- Physical therapy for pregnancy aches and pains
- Pelvic floor therapy
- Postpartum exercise
- Exercise and massage for the newborn
- Parent-child organized play

Finding Prenatal Classes in Your Area

After you decide which topics interest you, use this list of resources to locate classes offered in your area. Collect information on the chart that follows.

Resources

- Your caregiver
- Hospital or birth center education department
- International Childbirth Education Association (ICEA) (To find an ICEA-certified educator in your area, call 952-854-8660, e-mail info@icea.org, or visit http://www.icea.org.)
- Lamaze International (To find a Lamaze-certified educator in your area, call 800-368-4404, e-mail info@lamaze.org, or visit http://www.lamaze.org.)
- American Academy of Husband-Coached Childbirth (AAHCC, sponsors of the Bradley Method) (To find a Bradley-certified educator in your area, call 800-4ABIRTH or visit http://www.bradleybirth.com.)
- Community-based pregnancy or parenting organization
- Your health insurance provider
- Friends, relatives, and colleagues
- Community education organization or community center
- YMCA or YWCA
- Health club
- City or county health department
- Local women's group
- College or university
- Maternity or baby store
- Local chapter of American Red Cross
- Place of worship
- Community bulletin board
- Community parks and recreation department
- Public library
- Telephone directory yellow pages (Look under *Child*, *Child Counselors*, *Child-Parent Development*, *Childbirth Education*, *Maternity Services*, or *Social Service Organizations*.)

Class Information

Class	Date(s)	Location	Enrollment Deadline	Cost	Contact Information

Choosing a Childbirth Class

Most childbirth classes cover basic information about birth and birth-related procedures. However, they vary in their philosophies, teaching methods, and formats. Some classes also cover breastfeeding and parenting a newborn. Classes offered by a hospital, birth center, or caregiver will provide information according to the policies and procedures of that facility or practice. Independent educators or childbirth education groups may promote a specific philosophy.

Class sizes and schedules also vary. When the class has no more than ten couples, it's easier to get to know one another and ask questions. A series taught over several weeks gives you time to practice the skills and develop relationships. A weekend class concentrates information into a short period, which may benefit couples who have scheduling conflicts. Private education can tailor a class to your specific needs.

To choose the childbirth class that's right for you, ask the following questions:

- What is the instructor's or organization's philosophy of childbirth?
- What topics does the class cover?
- How are classes organized?
- How much time is spent on lecture, discussion, and practice?
- What's the class schedule and location?
- How many participants are likely to be in the class?
- What's the maximum number of participants?
- What's the cost?
- Are there scholarships?
- Does the instructor or organization offer other kinds of childbirth or parenting classes?
- How are special circumstances accommodated?
- Is the instructor a certified childbirth educator? If so, by what organization?
- What other professional qualifications does the instructor have, such as nurse, lactation consultant, or early childhood development specialist?

Prenatal Exercise Guidelines

If you take a prenatal or postpartum exercise class, bear in mind the following guidelines from the American College of Obstetricians and Gynecologists (ACOG).

Recommendations

1. During pregnancy, mild to moderate exercise for thirty minutes or more is safe for most, if not all, days of the week.
2. After the first trimester, avoid exercising flat on your back. This position can cause dizziness and reduce blood flow to the uterus. Also avoid standing still for more than fifteen minutes at a time to encourage circulation and prevent varicose veins.
3. Pregnancy decreases the amount of oxygen available for aerobic exercise, so modify the intensity of your exercise accordingly. Stop exercising when you're fatigued. You may be able to continue weight-bearing exercises throughout pregnancy, but non–weight-bearing exercises like swimming pose less risk of injury.
4. Don't do any exercises that could make you lose your balance, especially in the third trimester, and avoid any exercises that may cause even mild abdominal trauma (like stomach crunches).
5. Pregnancy requires extra calories, so make sure to eat a good diet if you're exercising.
6. When exercising during the first trimester, drink lots of water, wear cool clothing, and exercise in an environment that's not too warm.
7. After your baby's birth, lose the weight you gained during pregnancy gradually.

Contraindications

You should not exercise during pregnancy if you have:

- Hemodynamically significant heart disease
- Restrictive lung disease
- Incompetent cervix or cervical cerclage
- Multiple gestation at risk for premature labor
- Persistent second- or third-trimester bleeding
- Placenta previa after twenty-six weeks
- Premature labor
- Ruptured membranes
- Pregnancy-induced hypertension

Consult with your caregiver before exercising if you have:

- Severe anemia
- Unevaluated maternal cardiac arrhythmia
- Chronic bronchitis
- Poorly controlled type 1 diabetes
- Extreme obesity
- Extreme underweight
- History of extremely sedentary lifestyle
- Intrauterine growth restriction
- Poorly controlled hypertension or preeclampsia
- Orthopedic limitations
- Poorly controlled seizure disorder
- Poorly controlled thyroid disease
- Heavy smoking habit

Stop exercising and contact your caregiver if you experience:

- Vaginal bleeding
- Difficulty breathing
- Headache
- Chest pain
- Muscle weakness
- Calf pain or swelling
- Preterm labor
- Decreased fetal movement
- Leaking amniotic fluid

Prenatal Testing

Throughout your pregnancy, your caregiver may order various prenatal tests. Some tests check for maternal health; others check for fetal health and development. The following section describes the most common prenatal tests. Ask your caregiver for more specific information.

Routine Exams and Tests

Pelvic Exam

First or second prenatal visit:

- To confirm pregnancy and estimate size of uterus
- To estimate size and shape of pelvis

- To obtain vaginal secretions to detect infectious organisms
- To screen for cervical cancer (Pap smear)

Late pregnancy:
- To assess condition of cervix and station (descent) of baby
- To obtain vaginal secretions to detect infectious organisms

Urine Test

First prenatal visit:
- To confirm pregnancy
- To screen for urinary tract bacteria

Each prenatal visit:
- To screen for sugar and ketones, which might indicate diabetes
- To screen for protein, which might indicate pregnancy-induced hypertension (PIH) or infection

As indicated:
- To detect infectious organisms
- To diagnose a urinary tract infection

Blood Test

First or second prenatal visit or later, if indicated:
- To confirm pregnancy
- To determine blood type and Rh factor or screen for antibodies in Rh-negative mother
- To test for anemia
- To test for infectious organisms or antibodies against them
- To evaluate blood glucose levels in women with diabetes mellitus

Blood Pressure Check

Each prenatal visit:
- To screen for high blood pressure, which might indicate PIH

Maternal Weight Check

Each prenatal visit:
- To detect sudden weight gain that could be due to PIH
- To monitor mother's nutritional status

Abdominal Exam

Each prenatal visit:
- To measure growth of uterus, which indicates fetal growth and gestational age

Each visit in last weeks of pregnancy:
- To estimate size and position of fetus
- To estimate amniotic fluid volume
- To detect breech presentation

Listening to Fetal Heart Tones (FHT)

Each prenatal visit after FHT can be heard (at about ten to twelve weeks):
- To check that the fetus is alive
- To check the heart rate for fetal well-being

Breast Exam

Once or more during pregnancy:
- To assess condition of breasts for breastfeeding
- To screen for breast cancer

Dental Exam

Once or twice during pregnancy:
- To check for tooth decay and repair, if necessary
- To clean teeth
- To check for gum infection

Multiple Marker Screening

At fifteen to twenty weeks:
- To screen for combinations of certain substances in the blood that could indicate Down syndrome or other disorders
- To screen for high levels of a substance in the blood that could indicate a neural tube defect or an increased risk of other fetal abnormalities or death

Glucose Screening

At twenty-four to twenty-eight weeks:
- To screen for gestational diabetes

Group B Streptococcus (GBS) Screening

At thirty-five to thirty-seven weeks:
- To screen for presence of GBS and identify women who are GBS carriers

Diagnostic Tests

Amniocentesis

Using ultrasound for guidance, the doctor passes a needle through the abdomen and uterus into the amniotic sac, withdraws fluid, and sends it to a lab for examination. Amniocentesis can be performed when there is an adequate amount of fluid.

In first or second trimester:
- Provides information on particular birth defects, metabolic disorders, and chromosomal or genetic diseases
- May detect Down syndrome, sickle cell anemia, neural tube defects, and many other disorders
- Provides more detailed information about fetus when results of screening test(s) suggest a problem

In third trimester:
- Provides information on fetal lung maturity when early delivery is being considered
- Reveals severity of Rh disease or other suspected blood disorders and helps determine if treatment of baby will be necessary

Biophysical Profile

This test estimates fetal well-being in the latter weeks of pregnancy to determine if a high-risk or a postdate pregnancy could safely continue or if labor should be induced. Each of its five components is scored with zero, one, or two points.

Non-stress test:
1. Fetal heart rate's response to movement

Ultrasound scan:
2. Fetal movement and activity
3. Fetal muscle tone
4. Fetal breathing movements
5. Amniotic fluid volume

Chorionic Villus Sampling (CVS)

Using ultrasound for guidance, the doctor passes a catheter through the cervix or a needle through the abdomen and uterus, placing it on the chorionic membrane covering the fetus. Tiny pieces of the chorionic villi are suctioned into a syringe and sent to a lab for analysis. CVS is usually performed at ten to twelve weeks.

- Provides information about chromosomal abnormalities
- Provides information similar to amniocentesis, but earlier in pregnancy
- Provides sample large enough for DNA analysis

Contraction Stress Test or Oxytocin Challenge Test

This test shows how the fetal heart rate (FHR) responds to uterine contractions. Contractions are induced until the mother has three contractions in ten minutes. Then, while the uterus continues contracting at that rate, an external electronic fetal monitor measures the FHR. Test results are "reassuring" if FHR remains normal during contractions. Results are "ominous" if FHR indicates fetal distress.

- Predicts whether fetus can withstand stress of labor
- Helps decide if high-risk pregnancy can continue, if labor should be induced, or if cesarean birth is indicated
- Estimates placental function and fetal reserves

Cordocentesis or Percutaneous Umbilical Blood Sampling (PUBS)

Using ultrasound for guidance, the doctor passes a needle through the mother's abdomen and uterus into the umbilical cord and withdraws fetal blood for testing. This test can be performed after sixteen to eighteen weeks.

- Assesses fetal blood to detect anemia and oxygen level
- May be used to give a blood transfusion, administer medications, or monitor effectiveness of fetal drug treatment

Doppler Blood Flow Study

A Doppler ultrasound unit placed on the mother's abdomen monitors the blood flow rate in the umbilical artery, the fetal blood vessels, and/or the mother's uterine artery.

- Helps identify fetal-placental circulation problems

Fetal Movement Counting

During the third trimester, the mother counts and records her baby's movements during a brief, specified period each day.

- Provides more reliable information than mother's informal impressions of fetal activity
- Helps assess well-being of fetus
- Helps mother learn about her baby

Glucose Tolerance Test

This test evaluates the body's ability to handle a large dose of sugar. The technician draws blood before the mother drinks a sugary drink and then again at one hour, two hours, and three hours afterward.

- Helps diagnose gestational diabetes if indicated by a screening test

Magnetic Resonance Imaging (MRI)

A superconductive magnet moves over the mother's skin above the area that is to be visualized. Composite images projected onto a video screen show different cross sections of the maternal or fetal organs or vessels being evaluated.

- Allows a detailed look at internal organs and vessels
- Estimates size of fetal anatomical structures and maturity of fetal organs

Non-Stress Test

The FHR is recorded for twenty to thirty minutes with an external electronic fetal monitor, and the mother indicates each time she feels the baby move. If there is no spontaneous fetal movement, the baby may be asleep. The examiner may push on the mother's abdomen or make a loud noise near her abdomen to stimulate the baby. An increase of fifteen beats above the base line heart rate for fifteen seconds while the fetus is moving is normal and a sign of fetal well-being.

- Predicts fetal well-being
- Helps determine if a high-risk pregnancy can safely continue or if further testing is desirable

Ultrasound (Sonography)

High-frequency sound waves are sent through a transmitter into the mother's uterus via the abdomen or vagina. These waves echo back from various structures of the fetus, the placenta, and the mother's internal organs to form a picture on a video screen. Timing depends on the reason for testing.

- Confirms pregnancy and number of babies
- Helps estimate fetal age by measuring the skull, femur, crown-rump length, or other landmarks
- Helps estimate fetal growth and weight
- Helps locate fetal organs and structures for inspection, measurement, diagnosis, or treatment
- Helps assess position and condition of placenta and cord
- Detects fetal presentation and position
- Helps assess amniotic fluid volume
- Helps evaluate fetal characteristics and amniotic fluid volume for biophysical profile
- Helps confirm diagnosis if other testing suggests a problem
- Measures cervix to determine effacement

Vaginal/Cervical Smear

At any time during pregnancy, secretions from the mother's vagina or cervix can be obtained with a swab or suction bulb and then examined in a lab.

- Detects organisms that cause infections
- Determines whether membranes have ruptured
- May be used to determine fetal lung maturity, if membranes have ruptured
- Measures level of fetal fibronectin, which may help identify risk for preterm labor

X-ray

Ionizing radiation is used to take an internal picture of the mother and the fetus.

- Helps estimate size and shape of mother's pelvis
- Helps discover fetal position and presentation and number of babies

Genetic Counseling

Should You Talk with a Genetic Counselor?

You may benefit from genetic counseling if:

- You'll be thirty-five years old or older on your due date.
- You, your baby's father, or a blood relative of either of you has a genetic disorder, birth defect, or developmental delay.
- You or your baby's father has had genetic testing that indicates your baby could inherit a genetic disorder.
- The baby's father is your close blood relative.
- You've had a stillbirth, three or more unexplained miscarriages, or a child who died in infancy.

- Your ethnic background puts your baby at a higher risk for a genetic disorder, such as Tay-Sachs disease or sickle cell anemia.
- You have a medical condition that may affect your baby's health or require you to take medications or undergo treatments that may affect your baby's health.
- During this pregnancy you've been exposed to substances that may cause birth defects, such as radiation or toxic chemicals; you've had an infection that may cause birth defects, such as rubella, chickenpox, or cytomegalovirus (CMV); or you've used alcohol or drugs.
- You've had a prenatal test that shows a possible problem or a positive diagnosis of a genetic disorder in your baby.
- You're worried about your chances of having a child with a birth defect or genetic disorder and you want to know more about the available testing.
- Any of the preceding points describes you, and knowing more would help you choose a course of treatment, prepare better for your baby's needs, or decide whether to continue your pregnancy.

Questions to Ask Your Genetic Counselor

A good genetic counselor will provide much of the information suggested by the following questions without being asked. Still, it's wise to be prepared for your meeting so you can make the best use of your time together. Use this checklist to make sure you discuss all the issues important to your particular situation.

- What is the risk assessment or diagnosis for me?
  For my baby?
- Is there a test to determine whether a person has or carries this condition?
- Is there a prenatal test for this condition?
- What other diagnostic procedures are recommended for this condition?
- Who performs and what exactly is done during each diagnostic test or procedure?
- What specific information does each diagnostic test or procedure provide?
- How long does it take to receive test results?
  How will I receive them?
- How accurate is each diagnostic test or procedure?
- What are the risks of each diagnostic test or procedure?
- What are the characteristics of this condition?
- How does a person get this condition?
- Is there a cure for this condition?
- What is the treatment for this condition?
- Are there any special pregnancy precautions for this condition?
- How do you care for a person with this condition?
- What are the estimated medical costs for a person with this condition?

- How is this condition passed from one generation to the next?
- Can a person carry this condition and pass it on without having the condition?
- How likely is it that other members of my family besides me or my baby (such as older children or siblings) will have this condition?
- Where can I get more information about this condition?
- What services are available for people with this condition?
- How can I contact other people or families in a similar situation?
- What research is being done on this condition? Where and by whom?
- Where can I get a second opinion?
- What specialists will I need to see?
- How will this diagnosis affect my health insurance?
- When would it be appropriate to meet with you again?
- Additional questions: ______________________________

Questions for Your Health Insurance Provider

Genetic counseling and testing are often, but not always, covered by health insurance. Your coverage depends on your policy and your reason for counseling or testing. Call the customer service phone number on your insurance card and ask any of the following questions that concern you.

- How are genetic services defined?
- What coverage is provided for genetic services?
- Do I need a referral to see a genetic services provider? What is the process?
- Can I have a list of participating genetic services providers? What are their qualifications and credentials?
- Which family members can receive genetic services? Which services?
- What is the policy on previously unknown (asymptomatic) preexisting genetic conditions?
- If a genetic condition is diagnosed, is treatment covered? Which genetic conditions are covered or excluded? Does the plan cover medication, special formulas, or therapies (such as speech, physical, or occupational therapy)?
- How will my family's confidentiality be protected?
- Additional questions: ______________________________

Prenatal Testing Record

Test	Date	Caregiver and Facility	Results Date	Contact Information	Results and Recommendations

Preparing a Birth Plan

Preparing a birth plan will help you examine labor, birth, and baby care options, think about your preferences, and convey your wishes to your healthcare provider and all who will attend your baby's birth.

The following list presents common labor, birth, and postpartum healthcare practices. Discuss these options with your partner and your healthcare provider, tour your birth site, and share thoughts with friends and childbirth education classmates. Then complete your birth plan (page 81) with your preferences and make a copy for yourself, your partner, your caregiver, your nurses, your doula, and anyone else who may need one. Make a backup copy in case one is misplaced. Be sure to bring your copy and a backup with you to your birth site.

Keep in mind that each birth is unique, and that your birth plan is a statement of preferences, not an agenda or a contract. Circumstances may require deviation from your plan for the safety of you and your baby. Also, some options may be restricted by state law or hospital policy.

Common Healthcare Practices

Normal Delivery and Birth

During Labor

Support people and witnesses
- Partner
- Doula
- Friends or relatives
- Children (during labor and/or birth)

Vaginal exams
- At caregiver's discretion
- At mother's request or if needed for clinical decision
- Examiners

Labor positions
- Caregiver's choice
- Freedom to change positions, stand, and/or walk around
- Postural aids (birth ball, tub, beanbag chair, or other)

Food and fluids

- Eat and drink as desired
- Clear fluids (water, juice, Popsicles) by mouth
- Ice chips only
- Saline or heparin lock
- IV fluids

Emptying bladder

- Walk to toilet
- Bedside commode
- Bedpan
- Catheter

Monitoring fetal heart rate

- Auscultation with fetoscope or stethoscope
- Auscultation with Doptone (ultrasound stethoscope)
- Intermittent external electronic fetal monitoring
- Continuous with telemetry
- Continuous electronic monitoring (internal or external)

Pain relief

- Medications and medical procedures
  - Systemic medications
    - Sedatives and hypnotics
    - Tranquilizers
    - Inhalation analgesia
    - Narcotic or narcotic-like analgesics
    - Narcotic antagonists
  - General anesthesia
  - Regional and local analgesia and anesthesia
    - Standard epidural block
    - Segmental ("light") epidural block
    - Epidural or spinal (intrathecal) analgesia with narcotic or narcotic-like drugs
    - Epidural or spinal (intrathecal) narcotics followed by epidural anesthetic ("caine" drug)
    - Spinal (intrathecal) block (with "caine" drug)
    - Sterile water block
    - Paracervical block
    - Pudendal block
    - "Local" perineal block
- Nonmedical comfort measures
  - Emotional support from partner, friends, doula, and/or staff
  - Relaxation, breathing, focusing, and/or visualization

- Positioning, changing position, walking, rocking, and/or counterpressure
- Hot or cold compresses
- Water therapy (bath, whirlpool, or shower)
- Massage, acupressure, or acupuncture
- Hypnosis
- Aromatherapy
- Music

During Birth

Position for pushing and birth
- Mother's choice
- Caregiver's choice

Expulsion techniques
- Spontaneous bearing down
- Directed pushing
- Prolonged pushing

Promoting descent and delivery
- Gravity-enhancing positions
- Prolonged pushing on command
- Episiotomy
- Forceps or vacuum extraction

Bed/equipment for pushing/birth
- Choice of birth stool, beanbag, bathtub (water birth), floor, or bed
- Birthing bed
- Delivery table with or without stirrups

Covering the perineal area
- Undraped, mother may touch baby during birth
- Drapes around vagina and on abdomen and legs

Episiotomy
- Measures to help maintain intact perineum and to avoid a tear (warm compresses, pressure, controlled pushing, positions)
- No episiotomy
- Decision left to caregiver
- Anesthesia before episiotomy
- Anesthesia after birth for stitches

Postpartum

Cord cutting
- Partner or other support person cuts cord
- Caregiver cuts cord
- Clamp and cut after cord stops pulsating
- Clamp and cut immediately

Delivery of placenta
- Spontaneous
- Encouraged with breast stimulation, suckling
- Hastened with medication or fundal massage
- Upright position
- Manual extraction
- Use of placental tissue by the hospital

Maintaining uterine muscle tone
- Breastfeed baby
- Fundal massage by nurse or mother
- Medication to contract uterus

Immediate care of baby
- In parents' arms for observation and Apgar score
- In mother's bed for observation and Apgar score
- Near parents in bassinet or isolette
- In mother's bed for observation, weighing, and first bath
- In nursery for observation, weighing, and first bath

Warmth of baby
- Baby skin-to-skin with mother, with blanket or heater over both
- Wrapped in heated blanket, held by parent
- In heated bassinet in mother's room
- In special heated unit in nursery

Airway
- Suction only if necessary
- Suction with bulb syringe almost immediately

Vitamin K
- Oral doses
- By injection soon after birth

Eye care
- None
- Use of nonirritating antibiotic agent
- At one hour after birth

Cord blood collection
- Not planned
- Public cord blood bank donation
- Private or family cord blood collection and storage

Infant feeding
- Breastfeeding within first hour
- Breastfeeding, but could be delayed
- Infant formula
- Feeding on cues from baby
- Feedings scheduled by hospital staff
- Supplemental feedings to breastfed baby (water, glucose water, formula)
- Supplement (if used) given to breastfed baby by parents or nurse

Contact with baby
- Continuous rooming-in
- Daytime rooming-in
- For feedings only, in nursery at other times

Circumcision
- None
- Immediately (within two days)
- Delayed (within two weeks)
- With one or both parents present to comfort baby
- With no anesthetic
- With anesthetic
- At religious ceremony performed by spiritual leader

Newborn exam
- Performed by baby's caregiver
- Performed by hospital caregiver
- Performed in presence of parents
- Performed in nursery away from parents

Newborn vaccinations
- None
- Hepatitis B

Controlling pain

- Use of self-help techniques before use of medications
- Medications

Visitors

- Unlimited visitation desired
- Limit who will visit
- Limit when visitors can come into room
- Hours or amount of time limited by hospital

Dietary preferences

- General diet
- Vegetarian (lacto-ovo or vegan)
- Kosher
- Food allergies and sensitivities
- Other

Educational needs

- Breastfeeding
- Formula-feeding
- Baby care
- Maternal care
- Other

Follow-up with hospital staff after discharge

- Clinic or home visit with maternal-newborn nurse
- Breastfeeding help and support
- Phone call to or from hospital nurse

The Unexpected

If problems develop before or during labor, you may have to let go of some of your preferences, because more interventions may be necessary for safety. Consider the following options commonly available in such circumstances.

Unexpected Labor Events

Induction

- Avoid induction
- Induce at mother's or caregiver's convenience
- Non-drug methods
  - Sexual intercourse, orgasm
  - Nipple stimulation

- Enema
- Acupuncture or acupressure
- Stripping membranes
- Cervical dilators
- Artificial rupture of membranes
- Herbs and drugs
  - Herbal preparations
  - Homeopathic solutions
  - Castor oil
  - Prostaglandins
  - Synthetic oxytocin

Prolonged active labor
- Walk, change positions, take a bath
- Non-drug methods
- Herbs and/or drugs

Prolonged pushing
- Time spent before interventions
- Rest from pushing
- Change positions
- Directed pushing
- Pitocin
- Vacuum extractor, forceps, and/or episiotomy

Maternal exhaustion
- Rest, relaxation skills
- Bath, dim lights, privacy
- Drugs to aid relaxation or sleep

Suspected fetal distress
- Mother changes position, uses oxygen
- Fetal scalp stimulation to evaluate fetal well-being
- Amnioinfusion
- Continuous electronic fetal monitoring, internal scalp electrode
- Cesarean

Cesarean

Timing of planned cesarean
- After labor begins
- Scheduled before labor begins

Support people

- No support people present
- Partner only
- More than one support person
- Support person seated at mother's head
- Support person stands and watches or photographs surgery and birth

Anesthesia

- Regional anesthesia with or without premedication
- General anesthesia

Participation by mother

- Mother watches delivery of baby (window in screen or screen lowered)
- Anesthesiologist or obstetrician explains events during surgery
- No explanation of events

Postoperative medications

- At mother's request only
- Medications for anxiety, trembling, or nausea at anesthesiologist's discretion

Contact with baby

- Baby held by partner near mother soon after birth
- Baby held by mother during surgical repair of incisions
- Baby taken to nursery for well-baby observation
- If baby goes immediately to nursery or intensive care, partner goes with baby or stays with mother

Unexpected Developments with Newborn

If problems develop after the birth, you'll need to have a plan for these events.

Premature or Sick Newborn

Contact with baby

- Parents visit baby in special care nursery as desired
- If baby is transferred to different hospital than mother, partner goes with baby
- Kangaroo care for premature baby
- Parents feed and care for baby as much as possible

Feeding when baby can swallow food

- Mother breastfeeds baby, if possible
- Mother pumps breast milk and feeds baby by tube or bottle
- Formula-feeding by parents or nurse

Medications and procedures
- Parent involvement in decision-making and procedures
- Availability of staff for updates to parents

Contact with support group
- Initiated by parents, nurses, or support group
- No contact desired

Stillbirth or Neonatal Death

Medication for mother before, during, or after childbirth
- None
- At mother's request
- At caregiver's suggestion

Mother's participation
- Use of labor-coping techniques (with or without pain medication)
- Involvement in decision-making
- Labor management left to hospital staff

Mother's recovery and support
- Recovery on maternity unit
- Recovery away from maternity unit
- Early discharge
- Spiritual and grief counseling
- Later contact with parent support group
- Amount of supportive care from outside sources

Contact with baby after death
- See and hold baby after death
- No contact with stillborn baby

Care of baby after death
- Spiritual services (baptism, memorial service, funeral)
- Autopsy
- Burial or cremation

Memories of baby
- Obtain mementoes (photos, locks of hair, foot- and handprint, silhouettes, baby's blanket and hat)
- No mementoes
- Name baby

Birth Plan

Name: ____

Due date: ____

Primary caregiver: ______________________________________

Birth site: ____

My support people will be: (name) ________________________,

(relationship/role) ______________________________________

(name) ____,

(relationship/role) ______________________________________

We understand that this birth plan isn't a contract or a guarantee of an uncomplicated labor. Its purpose is to introduce us and convey our preferences.

Introducing us: ____

____

____

____

Important wishes, issues, fears, or concerns regarding mother or baby:_____

____

____

____

Preferences for managing labor pain: ______________________

____

____

____

Preferences for Normal Labor and Birth

First stage of labor (positions, movement, comfort measures, and food and beverages): ______________________________________

____

____

____

Second stage of labor (positioning and pushing): ______________

____

____

____

Third stage and first hours after birth (for mother and baby): _________

____

____

____

Preferences for Unexpected Events

Induction and prolonged or complicated labor: ____________________

____

____

Cesarean birth: ____________________

____

Premature or sick baby: ____________________

____

Stillbirth or death of baby: ____________________

____

Preferences for Postpartum in Hospital for New Mother

I plan to: ◇ Breastfeed ◇ Formula-feed

Concerns and questions: ____________________

____

____

Feelings about visitors: ____________________

Controlling pain: ____________________

Educational needs: ____________________

Follow-up after discharge: ____________________

Newborn Care Plan

Newborn care preferences for the baby of: ____________________

Baby's name: ____________________

Baby's doctor: ____________________

Infant feeding: ◇ Breast milk ◇ Formula

Newborn concerns, issues, wishes, and/or fears: ____________________

____

My previous experience with newborns: ____________________

____

Preferences regarding newborn examinations and procedures (vaccination, circumcision, contact with baby, and routine procedures): ____________________

____

____

Preferences for unexpected problems for the baby: ____________________

____

Educational needs (infant care, feeding, and so on): ____________________

____

Chapter Three

Mother's Needs

Maternity Clothing

You're dressing for two now, but it doesn't necessarily mean you'll have to purchase a whole new wardrobe. Friends and relatives are usually glad to lend or give away maternity clothes, and affordable secondhand maternity clothes are easy to find at consignment shops and thrift stores.

Practical Pregnancy Wardrobe Tips

These tips will help you assemble a pregnancy wardrobe that's comfortable, attractive, and affordable.

- Identify three favorite prepregnancy pieces, then find similar styles and colors when shopping for or borrowing maternity clothes.
- Make sure your maternity wardrobe includes a few neutral basics and colors that flatter you. Choose pieces that will mix and match with just about anything.
- Don't buy all your maternity clothes at once. You don't know exactly how your size and shape will change as time passes, nor what specialty items or pick-me-ups you may need later.
- Choose maternity clothes in the same size as your regular clothes. Such clothes will fit your basic body structure, which remains the same, but will allow more room in the belly, bust, hips, and armholes.
- Though you will probably need new underwear, you needn't buy maternity underwear, which can be expensive, unflattering, and—ironically—even uncomfortable. Low-rise cotton briefs are cheap, and they fit because the waistband rests under your belly instead of around it. You may find that hipsters work well in the second trimester and bikini briefs are best in the third.
- If you need to buy new bras and you're planning to nurse your baby, get nursing bras. Cotton-knit sports-style nursing bras are comfortable and adaptable to your ever-changing body.
- Because your hormones are raging and your blood volume's up, you're bound to be warmer than usual. Also, your pregnancy will span three seasons. Dress in layers so you can shed or add clothes easily throughout the day to stay comfortable. Soft, natural, breathable fabrics will provide the most comfort.
- Because your maternity wardrobe's smaller than your regular one, you'll be cycling through it faster. To save yourself money and hassle, choose durable, wash-and-wear clothing. Avoid clothes that need drycleaning or ironing.
- Don't be afraid to wear clothes that call attention to your belly. Show off your pregnancy if you like—it's something to be proud of, and the days of keeping pregnancy under wraps are over.

- Comfortable shoes are important not only for happy feet, but also for avoiding all-over aches and pains. Skip the heels except for the occasional special event, and invest in a pair or two of comfortable, attractive, low-heeled shoes if necessary. Buy shoes in the afternoon, when your feet are at their largest.
- When you buy new maternity clothes, be sure to try them on and ask about the store's return policy. Many maternity stores have a no-returns policy or will only allow exchanges or returns for store credit.
- Your pregnancy wardrobe needn't be exclusively maternity clothing. You may find the following nonmaternity clothes useful during early pregnancy and postpartum:
  - Sweatsuits
  - Bib overalls
  - Waistless dresses and jumpers
  - Blouses (With just the top buttons closed, you can wear these under bibs. Or don't button them at all, and wear them over a T-shirt or tank top.)
  - Men's button-down shirts
  - Wraparound skirts
  - Pants with elastic waistbands

Borrowed Maternity Clothing Organizer

Use the following chart to keep track of borrowed maternity clothes. First make sure the tag of each item is labeled with the owner's initial(s). Then record each article, including its color, owner, and condition, on the chart. Maternity outfits may come to you directly from other borrowers, and the owners may be unaware of their condition. Documenting problems like stains, rips, missing buttons, broken zippers, and worn elastic can prevent hurt feelings later on.

Article	Color	Condition	Owner

Clean the borrowed clothing, repair any damage, and return it toward the end of your pregnancy. After your baby arrives, you'll be too preoccupied. Remember the lender with a small gift for her or her child.

Taking Care of Mom

Handy Items for Mom

The following items are neither typical nor essential baby gear, but they can make your life as a new mom a lot easier and more pleasant.

Item	Advantages	Have	Want
Hand-held shower nozzle	Soothing for sore perineum and useful for washing baby's hair.		
Hand-held heat lamp	Soothing for sore perineum.		
Cordless phone	Helpful for taking and making calls from anywhere in your home or yard. Consider buying one with multiple handsets, each of which features caller ID, and only one of which needs a phone jack. You can keep a handset on each floor of your home and screen calls without running to the phone base. A hands-free (speakerphone) feature is useful for multitasking.		
Cell phone	Enables immediate communication in case of emergency, no matter where you are.		
Additional phone services (caller ID, call waiting, call forwarding, voice mail)	Handy for screening calls, catching expected calls, and taking messages.		
Home computer with Internet and e-mail capability	Helpful for communicating with others on your own time, sharing photos, researching parenting issues, and shopping online.		
Video camera	Useful for recording your baby's growth and making gifts for relatives.		

Item	Advantages	Have	Want
Home entertainment (Cable TV; DVD player; VCR; video, DVD, or book club membership; hobby)	Flexible, home-based activities can help you get some grown-up relaxation even while caring for an infant.		
Clock radio with timer for your and/or your baby's bedroom	Music can help settle your baby or gently awaken a sleepy newborn for feeding. Also useful for timing nighttime nursing sessions and shedding soft light in a dark room.		
Reading pillow with side arms	Provides arm and back support for nursing upright in bed.		
C-shaped nursing pillow	Provides arm support and encourages comfortable posture while nursing upright. Also handy for propping baby who's developing head, neck, and trunk control or learning to sit up.		
Penlight or miniature flashlight	Great for checking on baby or finding items in a dark room without waking baby.		
Hand-held digital recorder	Handy for recording special events such as your baby's birth, keeping an audio journal or to-do list, or tracking your baby's language development. You can also record yourself reading stories or singing songs for your child to listen to when you're apart. When memory is full, contents can be erased or transferred to a CD.		
Blow dryer	Set on low and held ten to twelve inches from the perineum or baby's bottom, a blow dryer can help heal a perineal tear or incision or a diaper rash.		

Item	Advantages	Have	Want
Intercom, baby monitor, or walkie-talkies	Let you keep an ear (and, with a video-style monitor, an eye) on your sleeping baby without visiting the nursery every few minutes. Two-way feature is useful for soothing a distressed baby as you make your way to the nursery or for easy communication with family members elsewhere in the home or yard. (Note: Some phones come with an intercom, paging, or walkie-talkie feature.)		
Back-seat mirror	Mounts on back-seat headrest so you can see a rear-facing baby's face while driving.		
Sunshades for car windows	Keeps sun out of your baby's eyes, which makes car rides more pleasant for everyone.		

Mom's Medication and Hygiene Organizer

Consult with your caregiver for recommendations about the personal care items in the following list. Consider stocking up on these items before your baby is born to reduce stress and add comfort to your postpartum recovery.

Item	Comments	Have	Want
Over-the-counter analgesics (ibuprofen and acetaminophen)	For general postpartum pain relief.		
Analgesic spray	For perineal pain relief.		
Sitz bath	For perineal cleansing and healing. Many hospitals provide you with a take-home sitz bath. If your hospital doesn't, buy or borrow one and learn how to use it in your bathroom.		

Item	Comments	Have	Want
Premoistened witch hazel pads	For perineal healing and comfort.		
Squirt bottle	For cleansing of perineal stitches. Hospitals often give one to new mothers to take home.		
Foam ring	Useful as a sitting aid.		
Psyllium husk bulking agent (such as Metamucil)	Treats constipation and prevents straining of sore perineal tissues.		
Lanolin breast cream	For preventing and treating sore or cracked nipples.		
Nursing pads	Protect clothing from leaking breast milk.		
Sanitary pads	Protect clothing from lochia.		

Third-Trimester Treats

Consider treating yourself to some of the following relaxing and fun activities during the last weeks of your pregnancy. They'll take your mind off any discomforts or anxiety you may have and will help you enjoy what remains of your pre-baby life.

- Have your hair cut, colored, or styled. (Make an appointment for your due date so you'll have something pleasant to do—and something to show for it—if your baby shows no signs of appearing.)
- Treat yourself to a manicure, pedicure, facial, makeover, or massage. (Be sure your massage therapist is experienced with prenatal massage.)
- Go out for dinner with your partner or a close friend.
- Plan a ceremony to celebrate your baby's birth.
- Be the guest of honor at a baby shower.
- Go shopping.
- Work on handicrafts for your baby.
- Have friends in for a visit.
- Take in a movie, concert, or play. (Sit in an aisle seat toward the back.)
- Stage your own film festival with rented videos or DVDs.

- Visit your local art museum or gallery. (It may be awhile before you get another opportunity.)
- Read those new novels now, while you have the chance!
- Enjoy a day trip or an overnight or weekend getaway with your partner.

Chapter Four

Baby's Needs

Feeding

Many studies in recent years have shown how important breastfeeding is to the well-being of babies, mothers, and society. This has fueled a resurgence of breastfeeding in North America, which was a formula-feeding culture for several decades. Both options are open to you as a new mom in the new millennium. The following pages outline the primary benefits and drawbacks of both to help you make the best choice for your family.

Breastfeeding and Formula-Feeding Comparison

Breastfeeding

Pros

- Helps mom's uterus return to normal size by stimulating production of the hormone oxytocin.
- Burns maternal calories.
- Is economical—costs only as much as mom's appetite.
- Is convenient—baby's nourishment is always on hand and ready to eat.
- Is environmentally sound—requires no manufacturing or packaging and produces no waste.
- Is emotionally satisfying for mom and baby.
- Enhances mother-baby bonding.
- Provides milk that's all-natural, guaranteed safe, and made for individual baby.
- Makes traveling with baby easy.
- Protects mom against ovarian, uterine, cervical, and breast cancers.
- Protects maternal iron stores due to delay of menstruation.
- Protects mom against heart disease and osteoporosis.
- Ensures mom sits or lies down regularly to rest.
- Gives mom regular surges of the "happy, calming" hormone, prolactin.
- Provides optimum nutrition for baby: Breast milk contains just the right amount of fatty acids, lactose, water, and amino acids for proper human digestion, brain development, and growth.
- Promotes optimum emotional, cognitive, behavioral, and physical development of baby.
- Results in less stinky spit-up and bowel movements.

- Provides baby with antibodies that protect against infections of ears, lungs, stomach, and gastrointestinal tract.
- Protects baby against allergy development.
- Is easy to digest, which means less constipation, diarrhea, and gas in baby.
- Encourages baby's proper jaw and tooth development.
- Provides colostrum to newborn, which strengthens immunity against infection and disease and helps prevent jaundice.
- Lets baby decide how often and how much to eat, which can lower risk of childhood and adult obesity.
- Protects baby against a number of terminal and debilitating diseases, like sudden infant death syndrome (SIDS), childhood leukemia, Crohn's disease, meningitis, and juvenile diabetes.

Cons

- Must be learned. Mastering breastfeeding can be difficult for both mother and baby. *But support and guidance from knowledgeable, empathetic groups, professionals, and family and friends can help mothers and babies achieve and continue breastfeeding success.*
- May draw unwanted attention in public. *But with a little practice, it's easy to breastfeed discreetly. Plus, with more and more women breastfeeding, the sight of a woman breastfeeding in public is becoming more frequent and less shocking. In addition, federal and state lawmakers are currently passing laws that support breastfeeding in public (and in general).*
- May cause the mother physical discomfort, like cracked nipples and engorged breasts. *But these problems can be managed or prevented by proper positioning, frequent feedings or pumping, and beneficial routines like breast massage and nipple cream application.*
- Only the mother can breastfeed. *It's true that only mothers can feed babies at the breast. But today's breast pumps allow mothers to express and bottle breast milk anywhere easily and quickly, which lets others enjoy feeding babies mothers' milk and lets mothers maintain their expressing schedule—and nourish their babies with breast milk—after returning to the workplace.*
- May make it hard to tell how much the baby has eaten. *But if the baby is wetting four to six disposable (or six to eight cloth) diapers and soiling three to four diapers in twenty-four hours, then he or she is consuming an adequate amount of food.*

Formula-Feeding

Pros

- Provides adequate infant nutrition when mother's milk is unavailable.
- Can be fed to baby by anyone without mom's involvement.

Cons

- Is nutritionally inferior to breast milk. Today's formula is still missing about a hundred nutritional components found in breast milk.
- Provides no antibodies.
- Can't be guaranteed safe. Contamination may occur at the manufacturing plant, in the bottles, and on the nipples.
- Can be time consuming and inconvenient. Sterilizing and toting bottles and preparing and heating formula takes a lot of planning and time.
- Raises baby's risk of illness. For every seventy-seven breastfed babies needing medical care for illness, *one thousand* formula-fed babies require such care.
- Is expensive. The average American family spends nearly three thousand dollars per year to formula-feed a baby. This amount includes the cost of the formula, bottles, nipples, and expected medical visits to care for illnesses.
- Doesn't help the mother's postpartum physical recovery.
- Doesn't promote mother-child bond as effectively as breastfeeding.

Breastfeeding Tips

- Ask your childbirth instructor if the hospital has a lactation consultant to help you get started.
- Make sure the baby latches on to your breast properly for your comfort and baby's effective feeding.
- Know how to monitor your baby's intake and output so you become confident in your ability to nourish your baby.
- Get support to help you manage and prevent problems.
- Expose your nipples to air or light to toughen them. Let breast milk dry on your nipples to lubricate them and prevent infection.
- Consider purchasing the following supplies:
    - Nursing bras: Be professionally fitted at a maternity shop, and purchase the bras toward the end of your pregnancy.

- Nursing pads: Disposable nursing pads are available. Less-expensive alternatives include cut-up diapers and cut-up sanitary pads. Washable pads are also available at most maternity shops. Less-expensive alternatives include men's handkerchiefs, cut-up toweling, and dishcloths.
- Waterproof pads: Protect your mattress against stains created by leakage at night.
- Supplies for expressing milk:
  - Pump (electric or manual)
  - Bottles and nipples
  - Breast milk storage bags or bottles for freezing

- Practice nursing discreetly so you can feel confident and relaxed about feeding your baby whenever and wherever he or she is hungry. If you like, carry a small blanket for extra coverage when nursing in public.
- Wear clothes that are convenient for breastfeeding:
  - Separates (One-piece outfits, as well as some jumpers and overalls, require disrobing to nurse.)
  - Easy-care fabrics (You'll be more relaxed about nursing if you're not worried about wrinkles, stains, and so on.)
  - Prints (Patterns hide leaks better than solid colors.)
  - Soft, light- or middle-weight fabrics (Scratchy, heavy, or bulky fabrics can be difficult to maneuver and/or uncomfortable for you and baby.)
  - Stretchy fabrics (If a shirt has some elasticity, you can position it as you like, and it'll stay put.)
  - Loose or oversize shirts (You can drape the extra fabric as you like to provide coverage.)
  - Front-buttoning shirts or dresses (You can unbutton just a couple of bottom or middle buttons to nurse with minimal exposure.)
  - Any front-opening shirt that can be worn over another shirt (For example, in the winter, you might wear a zip-front vest over a turtleneck. To nurse, you unzip the vest and lift the turtleneck. The vest keeps your exposed midriff warm and provides side coverage when nursing in public.)
  - Clothes designed especially for breastfeeding, with strategic openings for easy and discreet nursing

Bottle-Feeding Considerations

Equipment

Choosing a Breast Pump

If you want to bottle-feed your breast milk to your baby, you'll need the following equipment:

- Breast pump
- Collection kit
- Storage bottles or bags
- Refrigerator or freezer

Various types of breast pumps are available for rental or purchase. Choose the one that best meets your pumping needs and fits your budget.

- *Manual* breast pumps use the hand, arm, foot, and/or leg muscles to move the mechanism that creates suction. Most manual pumps empty one breast at a time, though some can pump both breasts. These are the least expensive pumps, but also the least effective. They're best for occasional pumping.
- *Battery-powered* breast pumps are similar to manual ones. They, too, are hand-held and usually pump one breast at a time. They're a bit more expensive than manual pumps, but not much more effective. They do, however, minimize muscle fatigue, and they're compact and handy when you can't tote a large pump or won't have access to an electrical outlet. Some come with AC adapters. They're best for occasional pumping.
- *Electric* breast pumps are plugged directly into an electrical outlet. Most are designed for double pumping, and many have adjustable suction and cycling. Some are designed to look like purses, briefcases, or backpacks and include storage space for the collection kit and pumped milk. Adapters that plug into a vehicle's cigarette lighter are available for many models. You can even buy a special bra to use with an electric pump that lets you pump hands-free. These are the most expensive pumps, but also the most effective. They're best for frequent use.

Choosing Bottles

If you'll be bottle-feeding human milk or formula to your baby, you have a number of bottle and nipple styles to choose from. None is inherently superior, but your baby may prefer a particular nipple, and you may find that some bottle systems are more convenient for you than others. The following list outlines the advantages of various nipple and bottle features.

You may want to buy a sample of each style in the beginning, then let your baby and your budget help you decide which to stock up on.

Bottle Features

- Shape
  - *Straight* bottles are cheap and easy to clean.
  - *Angled* bottles have a forty-five–degree bend that keeps the nipple filled with liquid to reduce baby's air swallowing and makes it easier to hold a baby upright, which prevents liquid from washing into baby's middle ear (a cause of ear infections).
- Usage
  - *Reusable* bottles are economical and environmentally sound because they can be used throughout your baby's bottle-feeding stage and create no waste. They also allow accurate measurement of the bottle's contents.
  - *Disposable* bottles require less cleaning because the milk is drunk from a presterilized plastic liner, which is thrown away at the end of the feeding. This bottle type may minimize baby's air swallowing (and thus prevent gassiness) because you can squeeze air out of the liner before feeding; also, the liner collapses as baby feeds, which prevents additional air bubbles from entering.
- Size
  - *Four-ounce* bottles are practical for newborns, who may drink only a small amount at each feeding. They're also handy for storing expressed breast milk.
  - *Eight- or nine-ounce* bottles are practical for older babies with bigger appetites. They can be used for a baby of any age and are therefore more versatile and long-lasting.
- Other features
  - *Bubble-free* bottles are ideal for gassy babies who don't like disposables. They let air in through the bottom of the bottle, which prevents it from mixing with the milk and being swallowed. Because both ends screw off, cleaning is easy.
  - *Chambered* bottles are great for traveling with a formula-fed baby. They have separate compartments for premeasured powdered formula and water. At feeding time, you twist the top and the formula mixes with the water.
  - *Hands-free* bottles are useful in a pinch, when young multiples who can't hold bottles yet need feeding simultaneously, and there aren't enough hands on deck for the usual holding and cuddling. The bottle fastens to a car seat or stroller, and a tube extends from the top to a pacifier-like nipple.

Nipple Features

- Material
  - *Latex* nipples are softer and more flexible than silicone nipples.
  - *Silicone* nipples are firmer and hold their shape longer than latex ones. They're less porous than latex and thus less prone to bacteria. They typically last three to four times longer than latex. They're also heat resistant and can withstand dishwashers.
- Shape
  - *Bell-shaped* nipples are inexpensive and widely available.
  - *Flat-topped* nipples mimic the shape of a mother's nipple.
  - *Orthodontic* nipples are elongated, flat on one side, and indented in the center to encourage the tonguing action of breastfeeding. They may help reduce tongue thrusting and bite problems caused by standard nipples.
- Flow
  - Nipples come with varying numbers and sizes of holes for varying flow speed. Here's a quick guide to choosing the right flow.... Always use newborn nipples for a breastfed baby of any age. The following guidelines apply to exclusively bottle-fed babies. For a newborn, the nipple size is right if the milk drips steadily when you turn the bottle upside down. For older babies: If your baby is sucking hard, fussing, then sucking hard again, you probably need a faster-flow nipple. If your baby is sputtering and gulping, you may need a slower-flow nipple.

Formula

Formula comes in several different forms and many different compositions.. Discuss with your baby's caregiver which formula he or she recommends for your baby.

Composition

- *Milk-based* formula is made with cow's milk and fortified with vitamins, minerals, carbohydrates, and fats.
- *Soy-based* formula is made from soybeans and is also fortified with vitamins, minerals, carbohydrates, and fats. It's usually consumed by babies who are allergic to cow's-milk protein or are lactose intolerant.
- *Iron-fortified* formula is recommended for all babies from birth to twelve months to promote normal mental and physical development.
- *Hydrolyzed-protein* formula is cow's-milk–based, but with the proteins predigested. It's consumed by babies with severe protein sensitivity.

Packaging

- *Ready-to-feed* formula is premixed and ready to pour into a clean bottle. This is the most expensive formula, but also the most convenient.
- *Powdered* formula must be mixed with water. You can prepare one bottle of formula at a time.
- *Concentrated liquid* formula must be diluted with water before it's poured into a bottle.

Bottle-Feeding Checklist

- Are the bottles and nipples clean and sterilized?
- Is the milk fresh? Human milk can be kept fresh in the refrigerator for up to eight days and in the freezer (with a separate door) for up to four months. If you're using formula, note the day and time that the can was opened and the formula mixed. Follow the manufacturer's recommendations for mixing and storage.
- Is baby getting the proper amount of milk through the nipple? See the nipple flow guide on page 98.
- Have you positioned the baby so he or she isn't lying flat? A baby sucks in more liquid per gulp from a bottle than from the breast, so positioning your baby's head above the rest of the body will help prevent ear infections and aid in digestion.
- Did you change sides while feeding the baby? Doing so helps baby's eyes and neck develop properly.
- Do you have a burp cloth handy? Most babies do at least a little spitting-up, and it's nice to keep everyone as clean and dry as possible. Also, if you're using formula, it'll stain clothing.
- Is baby showing any signs of constipation that you should report to the caregiver? Signs include cramping; straining and discomfort with bowel movement; small, hard, and pebbly or wide and large stools; diarrhea-like liquid stool passing out around a retained solid stool; or an abdomen swollen with gas. (Note: Constipation is usually not a problem with babies who are fed human milk.)

Baby's Caregiver

Around the twenty-fourth week of your pregnancy, you'll be encouraged to select a caregiver for your baby. You'll spend a great deal of time at the caregiver's office for well-baby visits during the first year, so it's important that you trust, respect, and feel comfortable with him or her. The following list describes the education and training of various pediatric caregivers. Make sure the caregiver you choose is covered by your insurance plan.

Types of Pediatric Caregivers

Pediatrician

- Specializes in children's healthcare.
- Graduated from a certified medical school and completed a pediatric residency.
- May or may not be affiliated with a hospital.
- May or may not be board-certified in a specialty.
- May be a Fellow of the American Academy of Pediatrics (FAAP). An FAAP is board-certified and a member of this pediatric honorary society. Generally accepted as having very complete pediatric training.

Family Physician

- Provides care for the entire family.
- Spent several months in pediatrics as part of medical school and residency training.
- Refers seriously ill children to doctors with specialty training.

General Practitioner

- Received a Doctor of Medicine (MD) or Doctor of Osteopathy (DO) degree.
- Frequently consults with pediatricians.

Pediatric or Family Nurse Practitioner

- Registered nurse with additional training in pediatrics or family health.
- Usually works with a group of physicians or in a clinic providing well-child care and treatment of common illnesses.
- Refers serious problems to pediatricians.

Physician's Assistant

- Graduated from a two-year program that features clinical training of primary medicine, including pediatrics.
- Provides pediatric services under the supervision of a physician.

Naturopath or Other Alternative Practitioner

- Provides well-child care and emphasizes nonmedical treatment of illnesses.
- Refers seriously ill children to medical doctors.

Locating a Caregiver

You can find a caregiver using the following resources:

- Your own primary caregiver, if you intend to choose a pediatrician
- Birth center of a hospital or clinic, especially postpartum and nursery nursing staff: Nurses see the caregivers at work with both mothers and babies and can therefore give you excellent advice and information.
- Health insurance provider directory: Your selection might be confined to a specific group of healthcare providers.
- Friends with children: Parents usually have strong feelings about their pediatric caregivers. Consider both positive and negative comments.
- Online caregiver locators, such as the American Academy of Pediatrics (AAP) Pediatrician Referral Service at http://www.aap.org or the American Academy of Family Physicians (AAFP) "Find a Family Doctor" service at http://familydoctor.org.
- County health association or board of health
- *The Official ABMS Directory of Board Certified Medical Specialists* (available at your local library)
- Local chapters of caregiver associations, such as the AAP, AAFP, or the American Medical Association (AMA).
- Teaching hospitals
- Telephone directory yellow pages, under *Physicians*, *Family Practice*, or *Pediatrics*.

Caregiver Evaluator

It's important to interview your child's caregiver. Some caregivers accept only newborns into their practices, and it may be difficult to change caregivers if you're unhappy with the care your child receives. There may be a charge for a preliminary interview, but it's money well spent. A caregiver may credit your account for the amount of the interview fee if you choose his or her practice. Following are several questions you may want to ask a potential caregiver and a few to ask yourself after the interview.

Caregiver's name: ______________________________
Office address: ______________________________
Telephone number: ______________________________
Appointment date: ______________________________

Training, Experience, and Affiliations

When and where did you receive your medical training? ______________
Are you board-certified? ______ In what specialty? ______________
By which organization? ______________
Do you have a subspecialty? ______________
How long have you been in practice? ______________
At which hospital(s) do you have admitting privileges? ______________
Are you involved with a teaching hospital? ______________
(Caregivers associated with teaching hospitals are involved in the training of other caregivers and therefore remain current on medical developments.)

Medical Philosophy

How do you view the parent's role in a child's healthcare? ______________

____

____

What are your views on breastfeeding? ______________
Circumcision? ______________
Infant sleep? ______________
Vaccination? ______________
Working parents? ______________
Do you typically take an aggressive or watchful-waiting approach when treating sick kids? ______________

Standard Care

Will you examine my newborn at the hospital? ______ When? ______________
How soon after my baby's initial exam would you like to see my baby again? ______________
What does a well-child checkup include? ______________
How much time is scheduled for it? ______________
Will you typically test my child's developmental status or rely on my observations? ______________
How much time is scheduled for a sick-child visit? ______________
Do you provide information on child development? ______________
Do you recommend classes, literature, or other parenting resources or activities? ______________

____

Do you offer sample medications so we can try them before filling a prescription? ______________

Availability

What hours is your office open?____
When are you at the office? ____
Does your office have early, late, or weekend hours to accommodate working parents or sick kids in urgent need of care?__________________________
Do you have multiple offices? ____
Who covers for you when you're on vacation? __________________________
If I call with a question, how will my question be handled? ______________
Do you have a regular time of day when you take and make phone calls? ______
Do you answer any questions by e-mail? ________________________________
Do you have a twenty-four–hour answering service? ______________________
Can I call you at home? ____

Office Staff and Resources

Are you in a group practice? ______ If so, can I meet your colleagues?________
How long do you plan to continue at the current location? _______________
Are there any plans to add or remove caregivers from your practice?____________
What other professional staff are available at your office? ________________
____
What are their roles? ____
What diagnostic capabilities (such as x-ray equipment or a laboratory) are available on-site?____
Does your office have separate waiting areas for sick people and healthy people?____

Administrative Issues

How are well-child appointments scheduled?______________________________
How far in advance must I typically book an appointment?_________________
Does your office phone, mail, or e-mail appointment reminders? _________
What is the fee for a standard office visit? ______________________________
What are my payment options? ____
Is payment due at the time of visit, or will I be billed? __________________
Are vaccinations extra, or are they included in the office visit charge? ________
Will I be billed for missed or canceled appointments? ____________________
Does your office accept my insurance?__________________________________
How are insurance claims handled? _____________________________________

Questions to Ask Yourself

Was the caregiver on time for the interview? ______________

Did the caregiver ask you about your family health history? ______ Your plans after your baby's birth? ______ Your feeding intentions? ______ Your fears and anxieties? ______________

Do the caregiver's views on breastfeeding, circumcision, infant sleep, vaccination, and working parents match yours? ______________

Does the caregiver seem to expect parents to be knowledgeable consumers or accept whatever he or she says? ______________

Did the caregiver volunteer information or wait for questions? ______

Did the caregiver treat you with respect? ______________

Did you and your partner feel comfortable? ______________

Do the caregiver's personality, age, and gender suit you? ______

Is the office location convenient for your daily routine? ______ (That is, is it near your home, workplace, or daycare provider or along your commuting route?)

Is the office pleasant and clean? ______ Is the waiting area spacious and comfortable? ______ Are there many toys and books? ______

Does the caregiver schedule at least a half-hour for well-child checkups? ______ (This allows time for parental questions.)

Do appointments typically run on time? ____ (Ask parents in the waiting room.)

Do you like the other staff? ______________

Do there seem to be enough staff to meet patients' needs? ______________

Caring for Baby's Health

Baby's Medicine Cabinet

Ask your baby's caregiver for guidance on the use of baby care products. To help prevent irritation, drying, and allergies, baby toiletries should be free of alcohol, preservatives, strong fragrances, and other strong chemicals.

- Diaper barrier cream for everyday use (Avoid petroleum products, which may inhibit the skin's ability to remoisturize itself.)
- Diaper rash cream or ointment
- Baby soap
- Baby lotion
- Baby shampoo
- Baby oil
- Sunscreen (Barrier-type sunscreens containing zinc oxide or titanium dioxide are more protective and less likely to cause irritation than chemical sunscreens.)
- Citronella insect repellent (Avoid deet-based repellents, which are not recommended for young kids.)
- Cloth or disposable baby wipes
- Alcohol-based hand sanitizer (for quick hand washing after diaper changes)
- Cotton balls
- Cotton swabs
- Baby hairbrush
- Infant acetaminophen or ibuprofen
- Digital thermometer (For a newborn, use a rectal or axillary thermometer. An ear thermometer is appropriate after age three months.)
- Alcohol for the umbilical cord
- Nasal aspirator
- Cool-mist vaporizer
- Baby nail clippers or blunt-nosed manicure scissors (If using either makes you uneasy, use a soft emery board.)

Newborn Health Diary

Make a few dozen photocopies of the following diary page to record daily observations of your newborn's health during his or her first six weeks. Tracking your baby's eating, sleeping, waking, and elimination patterns and other notable behaviors and physical symptoms will help you ensure that your baby thrives by helping you spot possible problems. It'll also give you confidence in your parenting and help you get acquainted with your baby. The information you record will be useful to your baby's caregiver and will help you remember all the things you want to discuss. By keeping records instead of relying on your memory (which may not be at its best due to fatigue), you can provide more accurate information.

Date

As you record each day's observations, write the date in the space provided at the top of the diary page.

Diaper Clocks

Output reflects intake, so tracking wet and poopy diapers is the best way to assess whether your baby is getting enough to eat—especially when you're breastfeeding. Whenever you change a wet diaper, note the time and write a *W* in the corresponding spot on the rim of the appropriate diaper clock. Whenever you change a poopy diaper, write a *P*. At the end of the day, tally your baby's wet and poopy diapers and write the totals in the spaces provided.

Activity Clocks

Each bar on the activity clocks represents five minutes. Whenever you feed your baby, note the starting and ending times of the feeding and fill in the corresponding bars on the rim of the appropriate activity clock. If the feeding was a nursing session, write an *R* (for right) or an *L* (for left) next to the feeding to indicate which breast you offered first. (This will help you remember to offer the other breast first at the next nursing session.) If baby ate from a bottle, write the number of ounces eaten next to the feeding. With a different-colored pen or pencil, record your baby's sleep periods in the same way. The blank bars remaining represent your baby's awake (nonfeeding) periods. At the end of the day, tally the total number of nursing sessions and/or ounces eaten and the total hours of asleep and awake time in the spaces provided.

Notes and Questions

If you observe any notable behaviors or physical symptoms in your baby, record them in the space provided. For example, you might record a long crying jag, fever, unusual-looking diaper contents, rash, and so on. Similarly, if you think of a question you'd like to ask an expert (for example, your baby's caregiver or a lactation consultant), record it in the space provided.

Date______________

Diaper Clocks

Wet diapers:_____ Poopy diapers:_____

Activity Clocks

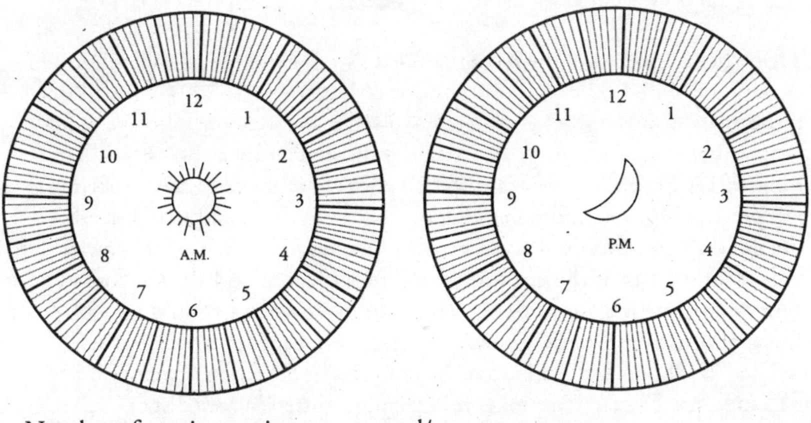

Number of nursing sessions:_____ and/or ounces eaten:_____
Hours asleep:_____ Hours awake:_____

Notable behaviors and/or physical symptoms: ______________________________

____

____

Questions: ____

____

____

Vaccinations

Recommended Childhood and Adolescent Immunization Schedule (United States 2003)

Vaccine ▼ / Age ▶	Birth	1 Mo	2 Mos	4 Mos	6 Mos	12 Mos	15 Mos	18 Mos	24 Mos	4–6 Yrs	11–12 Yrs	13–18 Yrs
Hepatitis B	HepB #1		HepB #2			HepB #3					HepB Series	
Diphtheria, Tetanus, Pertussis			DTaP	DTaP	DTaP			DTaP		DTaP	Td	
Haemophilus influenzae type b			Hib	Hib	Hib	Hib						
Inactivated Polio			IPV	IPV		IPV				IPV		
Measles, Mumps, Rubella						MMR #1				MMR#2	MMR #2	
Varicella							Varicella				Varicella	
Pneumococcal			PCV	PCV	PCV	PCV			PCV	PPV		
Vaccines below line are for selected populations												
Hepatitis A											Hepatitis A Series	
Influenza									Influenza (Yearly)			

Range of recommended ages

Only if mother HBsAg(-)

Preadolescent assessment

Catch-up vaccination

This schedule indicates the recommended ages for routine administration of currently licensed childhood vaccines, as of December 1, 2002, for children through age eighteen years. Any dose not given at the recommended age should be given at any subsequent visit when indicated and feasible. Black bars indicate age groups that warrant special effort to administer those vaccines not previously given. Additional vaccines may be licensed and recommended during the year. Licensed combination vaccines may be used whenever any components of the combination are indicated and the vaccine's other components are not contraindicated. Providers should consult the manufacturers' package inserts for detailed recommendations.

The Childhood and Adolescent Immunization Schedule is endorsed by:

- Centers for Disease Control and Prevention (http://www.cdc.gov/nip)
- American Academy of Pediatrics (http://www.aap.org)
- American Academy of Family Physicians (http://www.aafp.org)

More information regarding vaccine administration can be obtained from these organizations' websites or by calling the CDC National Immunization Hotline: 800-232-2522 (English) or 800-232-0233 (Español).

Keep track of your child's vaccinations with the CDC Childhood Immunization Scheduler (http://www.cdc.gov/nip/kidstuff/scheduler.htm).

Choosing a Name

Naming Considerations

One of the most important things you'll give your baby is a name. Consider the following factors when naming your child.

- **Namesake**—Does the name fit a child? An adult? Do you foresee any confusion with names ending with Jr., III, or a similar suffix?
- **Nationality**—Will a "foreign"-sounding name be easily pronounced and spelled by others? Does the name combine well with a surname if the two have different ethnic roots?
- **Religion**—Does your religion follow naming traditions? For example, some Roman Catholics prefer saints' names, and some Jews choose Old Testament names.
- **Gender**—Do you want a unisex name (for example, Robin, Chris, or Terry)? Or do you want a traditionally male or traditionally female name?
- **Number of names**—Keep in mind that most forms provide space for one first, one middle, and one last name.
- **Sounds**—Avoid a name that, when combined with a surname, creates a funny image or a rhyme (Rosie Butts or Tyrone Cohn, for example).
- **Rhythms**—Generally, a combination of first, middle, and last names that have different numbers of syllables creates a pleasing rhythm (for example, Molly Claire McDonald).
- **Pronunciation**—Will the name be pronounceable (based on its spelling) to a stranger?
- **Spelling**—Consider the consequences of a nontraditional spelling of a traditional name.
- **Popularity**—How will you feel about giving your child a popular name that many of his or her peers will likely have? Also, consider what your child may encounter if you select a very unpopular or odd name that no one else has (or wants).
- **Uniqueness**—Consider balancing the child's first and middle names by mixing a common name with a unique name (especially if the surname is very unique or very common).
- **Stereotypes**—Consider good and bad associations that come to mind with a particular name.
- **Initials**—Avoid combining names whose initials spell out an unfortunate word (for example, *DUD* or *HAG*).
- **Nicknames**—Keep in mind that your child may be called the nickname(s) associated with his or her name. If you choose a nickname as a legal name, your child may grow weary of explaining that the nickname is his or her full name.
- **Meanings**—Knowing the meanings of names can help you narrow your choices and select a winner.

Naming Worksheets

Favorite Names

Mom's Favorite Names

Girls' Names	*Rank*	*Boys' Names*	*Rank*

Dad's Favorite Names

Girls' Names	*Rank*	*Boys' Names*	*Rank*

Final Choices

Girls' Names

First	*Middle*	*Last*	*Rank*

Boys' Names

First	*Middle*	*Last*	*Rank*

Baby's Clothes and Linens

Your baby comes into the world wearing nothing but a smile, so you'll have to buy or borrow a lot of clothing to fully outfit your new little person for the first years. This section helps you weigh your diapering options, tells you the basic items you'll need, familiarizes you with baby clothing sizes, offers ways to make clothing last longer, and provides ideas for organization and storage.

The Diaper Debate

When it comes to clothing your baby, few issues are as onerous—and certainly none as odorous—as diapers. Here's a quick look at the advantages and disadvantages of the two main options: cloth diapers and conventional disposables. (Note: Some parents choose less-common options, such as "green" disposables or a diaper-free method called "elimination communication." For information on the former, check out manufacturers such as Seventh Generation (http://www.seventhgeneration.com) and Tushies (http://www.tushies.com). For info on the latter, see http://www.diaperfreebaby.org.

Diaper Comparison

Factor	Conventional Disposables	Cotton Diapers
Convenience	Easy to use. Fitted design helps prevent leaks. Can be tossed in any garbage receptacle. Must be emptied into toilet before disposal, though few users do this. Must be purchased regularly. Most daycare providers insist on disposables. Very absorbent.	Easy to use. (Velcro and snap designs have made diaper pins obsolete.) Must be used with moisture-resistant covers. Fitted designs help prevent leaks. Must be washed either at home or by diaper service. Must be emptied into toilet before washing. Must be stored until washed. Few daycare providers will use cloth. Less absorbent.

Factor	Conventional Disposables	Cotton Diapers
Cost	More expensive option.	Less expensive option if washing at home. Cost varies if using diaper service, but is usually comparable to or slightly less than disposables.
Environmental impact	Require large amounts of wood, plastics, energy, and water to manufacture. Manufacturing releases pollutants into environment. Fill up landfills and take hundreds of years to decompose. Leach chemicals into groundwater from landfills. Leach raw sewage into groundwater because few users empty into toilet before tossing.	Require fewer natural resources to manufacture. Are reusable. Require water and energy to wash, but less than used in manufacture of disposables. Require multiple washings and use of bleach if washed by diaper service. If washed at home, require no toxic chemicals (phosphates, bleach, and so on). Do not fill up landfills or contaminate groundwater.
Health	Contain sodium polyacrylate for absorbency, which is linked to toxic shock syndrome. Contain carcinogenic dioxin as a byproduct of bleaching. High absorbency may tempt users to leave dirty diapers on too long. Infrequent changes, perfumes, and other chemicals may contribute to diaper rash and allergic reactions.	Can be washed without leaving chemical residues that come into contact with baby's skin. Less absorbent material encourages more frequent changing, which may reduce diaper rash.
Comfort	High absorbency means baby feels drier. Paper product isn't as soft against baby's skin as cotton. Plastic outer covering does not breathe and traps heat.	Less absorbent material means baby feels wet when diaper is dirty. Wet feeling may encourage earlier toilet learning. Cotton is softer against baby's skin than paper products. Fabric diapers and covers breathe, helping baby stay cool.

Layette Organizer

Item	Approximate Number Needed	Number on Hand	Number to Buy or Borrow
Disposable diapers (if using exclusively)	150–200 for the first month		
Cloth diapers (if using exclusively)	2–3 dozen		
Moisture-resistant wraps for cloth diapers	3–6		
Diaper fasteners (for cloth diapers without Velcro or snaps)	3 one-piece clips or 3 pairs of clamps or pins		
One-piece pajamas or sleep sacks	4–7		
Side-snapping T-shirts (until the navel heals completely)	2–4		
Soft cotton shirts (with snaps at neck) or undershirts	4–7		
Onesies	4–8		
Stretchies or coveralls (outfits that cover baby neck to toe)	6		
Socks or booties	4–7		
Bibs	4		
Sweater or jacket	1		
Baby caps or wide-brimmed bonnets	1–3		
Snowsuit, bunting, or one-piece fleecewear	1		
Mittens	1 pair		

Item	Approximate Number Needed	Number on Hand	Number to Buy or Borrow
Receiving blankets	4		
Warmer blankets	2		
Fitted crib sheets	3–4		
Waterproof lap pads	3–4		
Waterproof mattress pads	1–2		
Washcloths	4		
Hand towels	4		
Hooded bath towels	2–4		
Other:			

Baby Clothing Sizes

Unfortunately, baby clothing manufacturers don't adhere to a standard sizing system. Some companies use the labels *small*, *medium*, *large*, and so on; others label their clothes by months of age; still others by weight. To make matters worse, the same term can mean different things to different manufacturers. When shopping for baby clothes, look for clothes labeled by weight, or take your baby with you so you can eyeball items for proper fit. If neither of these strategies is possible, use one the following charts to help you choose clothes that will (hopefully) fit your baby.

General Sizing

Size	Height	Weight
Newborn	up to 24 inches	up to 14 pounds
Small	24.5 to 28 inches	15 to 20 pounds
Medium	28.5 to 32 inches	21 to 26 pounds
Large	32.5 to 36 inches	27 to 32 pounds
X-Large	36.5 to 38 inches	33 to 36 pounds

Sizing by Age

Size	Height	Weight
0 to 3 months	up to 22 inches	up to 10 pounds
6 months	22 to 24 inches	11 to 14 pounds
9 months	24 to 25 inches	14 to 16 pounds
12 months	25 to 27 inches	17 to 20 pounds
18 months	27 to 30 inches	21 to 24 pounds
24 months	30 to 33 inches	25 to 28 pounds

Sleepwear Sizing

Size	Height	Weight
Newborn	up to 23 inches	up to 13 pounds
1B	23.5 to 26 inches	14 to 17 pounds
2B	26.5 to 29 inches	18 to 22 pounds
3B	29.5 to 32 inches	23 to 26 pounds
4B	32.5 to 35 inches	27 to 31 pounds

Baby Clothing Evaluator

The following checklist will help you choose baby clothes that are practical, safe, and comfortable.

Practical Features

- Long wrist and ankle cuffs to accommodate growing limbs
- Front opening, crotch opening, and/or encased elastic for easy dressing, undressing, and diapering
- Fasteners minimal and easy to manipulate
- One-piece design for speedy change of outfit
- Colorfast dye, including trim
- Machine washable and dryable fabric
- Wrinkle-free fabric
- Sturdy construction
- Full cut, extra limb length, and/or adjustable snaps for growing room
- Accessories (for example, matching bibs, vests, hats, or blankets) usable after baby has outgrown other parts of outfit
- Gender-neutral design that can be handed down to child of either sex

Safety Features

- No drawstrings, toggles, straps, sashes, or belts that hang loosely and pose strangulation hazards
- Roomy but not-too-loose fit (Loose-fitting coats and capes, and oversize or baggy clothing can get caught on furniture, in doors, and so on.)
- Flame-retardant fabric or snug fit for fire safety
- Absent or securely fastened bows, buttons, appliqués, and/or other trim to prevent choking
- No loose threads that could entangle baby's fingers or toes and cut off circulation
- Generous neck, arm, and leg openings for easy breathing and circulation
- Clearly identified manufacturer in case of questions, complaints, or recall

Comfort Features

- Seams flat, smooth, and minimal in number
- Absent or minimal trim
- Collars, buttons, bows, appliqués, snaps, and/or seams soft, nonbulky, and located where baby won't be lying on them
- Fit that's not too loose or too tight
- Soft, breathable fabric
- No features on inside of clothing (embroidery backing, zippers, stiff tags, and so on) that might irritate baby's skin

Stretching Your Baby Clothes Budget

Clothing a baby is a costly endeavor. New infant clothes are expensive, and it's hard to get your money's worth when your baby is growing like a weed and staining everything in sight or when the clothing isn't up to snuff. Following are some strategies for stretching your baby clothes budget by reusing clothes, buying smart, insisting on high quality, and caring properly for clothes.

Reusing Clothes

One great way to save money on baby clothing is to share with friends and save clothes for future kids. Boxes and bags of unmarked, unsorted clothing can overwhelm you, so use the following system to organize your borrowed and saved baby clothes.

Borrowed Clothes

1. Buy a set of permanent markers in a variety of colors.
2. Assign a color and an initial to each friend who has loaned you clothes.
3. Mark each article of borrowed clothing with the appropriate initial and color. (Double coding will help you determine the owner even after the marks have faded from frequent washing.)
4. Sort all clothing by size, disregarding ownership.
5. Place each size of clothing in a separate box. Number the boxes in ascending order, assigning the lowest number to the box of smallest-size clothes.
6. As your child outgrows the clothing, place all outfits (disregarding ownership) in a storage box.
7. Periodically sort the outgrown clothes and return them to their owners.

Saved Clothes

1. Mark baby clothing that you own and want to save with your initial only after your baby has actually worn it. (You might be able to return, exchange, or re-gift unused, unmarked baby clothes.)
2. Sort all clothing by size.
3. Place each size of clothing in a separate box. Number the boxes in ascending order, assigning the lowest number to the box of smallest-size clothes.

Buying Smart

- Buy baby clothes at consignment or thrift stores, where you'll often find high-quality, gently used items at great prices.
- Buy clothes on sale or at outlet stores.
- Buy big, and keep shrinkage from washing in mind when you buy.
- Choose multipiece outfits: They provide more flexibility. Larger pieces of the outfit can still be worn when smaller pieces do not fit.
- Buy clothes that allow for simple adjustments as baby grows larger; clothing that can be let out by snaps, straps, buckles, and cuffs.
- Cut the feet out of stretchies and have baby wear booties.
- Purchase clothing made of fabrics that give, like terry cloth and knits.

Insisting on High Quality

You're entitled to high quality in return for the money you spend on baby clothes. If an item doesn't withstand normal use, write the manufacturer. Many companies welcome consumer comments, which help the companies improve their products. Usually a manufacturer will replace a defective product. If a company doesn't offer to do so, suggest it in your return letter. Try the following steps when you find that you've bought poor-quality baby clothing.

1. If you have the receipt, return the item to the store where it was purchased. Suggest that the store management complain to the manufacturer, which will support your complaint.
2. Get the manufacturer's current mailing address. You can find this information on the Internet by searching for the company's name using any major search engine. You can also find print and electronic business directories at the public library. The consumer protection division of your state's attorney general's office should have information on businesses in your state.
3. Write a complaint to the manufacturer. Address the letter to the company's consumer complaint division, quality control department, or general office.
4. Be specific in your complaint. List the difficulties you've encountered (for example, elastic that's pulled away from the fabric, notions that have fallen off, snaps that have pulled loose, fabric flaws, bleeding dye, or poor seam construction).
5. Indicate how much wear or use the clothing has received. This is especially important if the clothing has been worn little and by only one child.
6. Include your full name and address as well as your telephone number and/or e-mail address. A company employee may contact you by phone or e-mail rather than surface mail to discuss your complaint. Be sure to date your letter, too, for easy reference in case the company does not respond and you need to send a second letter.

7. Make copies of all correspondence you send and receive. On your copies, note the date sent or received.
8. Send another letter if the first one is unsuccessful. Be more indignant in the second letter, conveying your anger about the quality of the company's clothing and about its attitude. Send a copy to the president of the company and, if the product is unsafe, to the U.S. Consumer Product Safety Commission (CPSC) at U.S. CPSC, Washington, DC 20207-0001 or info@cpsc.gov. Indicate on the letter that you're sending copies to the CPSC.

Caring for Baby Clothes

Your baby's clothing will get stained. Spit-up, pee, and poop are the main culprits. In general, these stains will be more stubborn if you formula-feed your baby. But don't despair: You may be able to save baby's clothing from permanent stains if you:

- Remember to follow the laundering instructions on the label.
- Treat stains immediately or at least before laundering.
- Choose clothing with patterns that hide stains.
- Launder clothes in cold water instead of hot water. (Cold water avoids permanently setting stains, minimizes fabric wear, limits dye bleeding, and reduces energy costs.)

Laundering Cloth Diapers

There are various methods for laundering cloth diapers, but here's a particularly easy, effective routine:

1. Set up a dry diaper pail (a plastic wastebasket with a flip-up lid, lined with a waterproof nylon laundry bag), and toss in the dirty diapers. Keep the lid closed to contain odors.
2. Run the diapers through one cold water rinse without detergent, then one hot wash cycle using a detergent without bleach (disintegrates fabric), fabric softener (ruins absorbency), or perfume (may irritate baby's skin). Toss in any diaper wraps that need washing during the hot cycle.
3. Machine-dry the diapers or hang them outside to dry. (Sunshine will bleach them naturally.) If line-dried diapers are stiff, toss them in the dryer and run the air-fluff cycle for a few minutes.
4. To dry the diaper wraps, lay them on top of the dryer while the diapers are drying inside, machine-dry them on the air-fluff cycle, or line-dry them. (Don't machine-dry them in a hot dryer; this may ruin them.)

Stain Treatment Chart

Post the following chart in your laundry room.

Type of Stain	Pretreatment	Washing Instructions
Protein stains (blood, spit-up, pee, poop)	Soak first in cold water, then rub stain under cold running water to dislodge the stain.	Launder in warm water with detergent.
Oil-based stains (petroleum jelly, ointment)	Pretreat with solvent-based stain removal product.	Launder in the hottest water that's safe for the fabric. Repeat if necessary.
Tannin-based stains (red berries, fruit juices, many medicines)	Pretreat medicine dye stains with heavy-duty detergent.	Launder with detergent (*not* natural soap) in the hottest water that's safe for the fabric. Medicine dye stains may require bleach.

Note: Consider a second rinse cycle on all loads to remove any detergent residue that could irritate baby's sensitive skin. Flame retardant (found on some sleepwear) can be removed with soap. Use laundry detergent or follow manufacturer's recommendations.

Baby Gear

What follows is a list of baby gear you'll probably need and explanations of your options, along with suggestions for cheaper alternatives and multiple-use items. You can save money by purchasing equipment with multiple uses, such as car seats that convert to strollers, or items that grow with a child, such as cribs that convert to juvenile beds.

Baby Gear Checklist

Gear	Options	Tips
Bed	Crib	A crib can be your child's bed until age two or older. When buying a new crib, look for one with a Juvenile Products Manufacturers Association (JPMA) certification safety seal. If using a secondhand crib, make sure the crib doesn't have missing, loose, broken, or improperly installed screws, brackets, or other hardware on the crib or in the mattress support. Make sure the space between crib slats is no more than 2⅜ inches wide, and don't use a crib with missing, broken, or loose slats. Check that the mattress is firm and fits snugly in the crib. (You shouldn't be able to fit two fingers between the mattress and the side of the crib.) And check that the mattress support doesn't pull apart from the corner posts easily. A safe crib won't have cracked or peeling paint, lead-based paint, splinters, or rough edges.
	Bassinet or cradle	Both are compact and portable, but baby will outgrow it by age four to six months. Look for a bassinet or cradle with a wide base, sturdy construction, and no rough edges. If choosing a folding model, check for secure leg locks or latches. If the model has wheels, make sure they lock. If the model has slats, the spaces between them should be no more than 2⅜ inches wide. Make sure the mattress fits snugly; you shouldn't be able to fit two fingers between the mattress and the side of the bassinet or cradle. If the model has a hood, make sure it folds back, or it'll get in the way when putting the baby inside. Bassinets and cradles can be toppled, so they may not be safe if you have other children or pets in the home.

Gear	Options	Tips
Bed *(continued)*	Bedside co-sleeper or compact infant bed	Both are perfect for co-sleeping families, promoting bonding and breastfeeding and perhaps preventing sudden infant death syndrome (SIDS). Some bedside co-sleepers can convert into freestanding bassinets, changing tables, and play yards. Compact infant beds allow a baby to safely sleep in the parents' bed. (See http://www.armsreach.com for more information on bedside co-sleepers, and see http://www.babydelight.com for more information about compact infant beds).
	Play yard	This convenient, portable product is great for travel because it can be used as a crib, bassinet, changing table, and play area.
Bedding	Fitted sheets	Whatever bed you choose for your baby, make sure the sheet fits tightly and securely around the mattress. Bumper pads aren't recommended (because they can suffocate the baby), but if used they should be thin and anchored tightly to the sides of the bed. Blankets are also a suffocation hazard; if used, they should be lightweight. A wind-up mobile can soothe baby to sleep, but make sure it meets safety standards.
Changing area	Changing table	Check that it's sturdy and has a high guardrail, secure safety straps, and a place to store diapers, wipes, and creams. (Open shelves are more convenient than small, high-sided baskets, but make sure the shelves are out of reach of crawling or walking children.) Be wary of ones with flip-open changing areas that extend beyond the main table. The table may topple when a baby is placed near the edge of the overhang.
	Combination dresser and changing table	Again, be wary of ones with flip-open changing areas that extend beyond the main dresser. The dresser may topple when a baby is placed near the edge of the overhang.

Gear	Options	Tips
Changing area *(continued)*	Rail rider changing table	This space saver attaches to the rails of a standard crib. When not in use, one end detaches, and the table hangs flat against the side of the crib. Check for stability and secure safety straps.
	Wall-mounted fold-out changing table	Here's another space saver that can be used for babies up to thirty pounds. Check for stability and secure safety straps.
	Play yard changing area	This removable pad attaches to the rails of a play yard. Check for stability and secure safety straps.
	Contoured changing pad	This thick, waterproof pad comes with safety straps and screws for attachment to a standard changing table. It can also be placed on the floor, dresser top, or elsewhere. If using on an elevated surface, make sure the surface is wide, sturdy, and at a comfortable height. Because you can't anchor the changing pad to the surface, be sure the surface is nonslip.
	Portable changing pads	Typically used on-the-go, these waterproof fabric squares or fold-up nylon, vinyl, or plastic changing kits can also be used at home. They're best used on the floor, since they usually don't come with safety straps.
Diaper pail	Diaper disposal system (for example, Diaper Genie)	This product is popular with parents using disposable diapers. It reduces odor and mess, but the system itself and its liner refills can be expensive.
	Flip-top diaper pail (with or without lock) or plastic wastebasket	*Disposable diapers*: You can use regular garbage bags as liners. A foot release allows you to open the pail with full hands. *Cloth diapers*: Many parents prefer to presoak cloth diapers in the pail (wet diaper pail). Others find soaking unnecessary and line the pail with a waterproof nylon bag (dry diaper pail).

Gear	Options	Tips
Chair for parent	Rocking chair, glider chair, recliner, armchair	You can use a traditional rocking chair, armchair, or recliner anywhere in the house long after your baby has grown. Gliders can be expensive and many are designed for nurseries only, but many parents swear by their comfort. If you'll be breastfeeding, special nursing pillows and footstools are available, but you can use regular pillows and footstools just as effectively.
Low light	Nightlight, lamp with dimmer switch	A dim light allows you to see in the nursery safely without turning on a bright light and disturbing a sleeping baby.
Bathtub	Baby tub, tub/sink liner	If buying a baby tub, look for one that's made of thick, sturdy plastic. Buy one that has a smooth, rounded lip; a padded, slip-resistant seat set at an angle comfortable for baby; a small indented section at one end for holding bath gear; and a plug at the base of the tub. A less expensive option is a tub or sink liner, a thick sponge that cushions baby in a sink or tub. A bath thermometer is a good safety purchase that's inexpensive.
Car safety seat	Infant car seat	Always rear-facing, designed for infants up to 20 or 22 pounds. Can be removed from base and attached to convertible strollers or carried by hand. Models come with either a three-point or a five-point harness.
	Convertible car seat	Rear-facing for infants until they are one year old *and* over 20 pounds, front-facing until the child has out grown the manufacturer's specifications. Models come with a five-point harness, a three-point harness with T-shield, or a three-point harness with overhead shield.
	All new car seats	Must meet the federal government's standards, but a car seat can still present safety problems if it's installed incorrectly or doesn't fit your child. Avoid buying a used car seat. Look for a new one with easy installation, adequate restraints, belt adjustments, tethers, washability, and a well-padded seat with plenty of head and back support.

Gear	Options	Tips
Stroller	Lightweight	Convenient and portable, but not designed for newborns.
	Standard	Sturdy and has reclining seat and storage room, but can be cumbersome and expensive.
	Convertible	Removable car seat is very convenient, but many models are pricey.
	Jogging	Can travel on all terrains, but aren't designed for newborns and can't fold up as compactly as standard strollers.
	Carriage	Have large wheels for smooth rides and can be quite fancy but also heavy, difficult to store, and very expensive.
	All strollers	Choosing the right stroller depends on your lifestyle. In general, look for a stroller with buckles and belts that are easy to fasten and adjust, an adjustable seat and canopy, washable fabric, an adjustable handle, an easy folding mechanism, brakes, wide wheel base, and swivel wheels. If using a secondhand stroller, check with either Consumer Reports (http://www.consumerreports.org) or the Consumer Product Safety Commission (http://www.cpcs.gov) to make sure the model hasn't been recalled. Make sure the used stroller is sturdy with smooth-rolling wheels and secure safety belts. Check for cracks or splits or sharp edges.
Carrier	Front carrier	Look for one that will support your baby securely and allow a choice of positions. Make sure all straps, buckles, snaps, and belts are durable. Look for wide, padded, adjustable shoulder straps; a padded waist/hip belt; a sturdy padded headrest; and leg holes banded with elastic or padded fabric. Make sure you can easily slip the carrier on and off. Check that the fabric suits the season.
	Sling	Make sure that the fabric won't smother your baby. A cotton sling is warm, soft, breathable, and machine-washable.

Gear	Options	Tips
Carrier *(continued)*	Backpack (for baby five to six months or older)	Look for one with wide, padded, adjustable shoulder straps and hip belt that don't slip. The lighter the pack is without the baby, the lighter it'll be *with* the baby. Look for a roomy, adjustable inside seat with an adjustable safety harness that clasps across the chest and shoulders. Choose a model with easily accessible compartments. Consider one with a protective canopy. Look for a model with a support stand that locks firmly.
	All carriers	Suit the style to your setting. Pouch-style carriers, particularly those made of corduroy or heavy-gauge nylon, may be too warm for the dog days of summer.

Nursery Decorating Tips

- Use nursery wallpaper border instead of nursery wallpaper. A border is usually cheaper and easier to change as a baby grows up.
- Cut large, bold geometric shapes from contact paper. Place these shapes on the wall, furniture, and ceilings.
- Decorate with functional items. If you receive several adorable crib blankets, hang them on the wall on curtain rods or tack them directly to the wall.
- If you receive any congratulatory plants or flower arrangements, keep the decorative pots and use them to store such items as cotton balls, hairbrushes, and toiletries.
- Make stuffed animals the room's focal point. Place the animals on shelves and in windows, or attach them to curtain rods. You can also suspend stuffed animals on ribbons from hooks on the ceiling or the wall.
- Decorate with gender-neutral colors and themes (for example, Noah's ark, teddy bears, clowns, ducks, bugs, rabbits, cartoon or fairy tale characters, alphabet letters, numbers, kites, balloons, clouds, stars and moons, or rainbows). Unless you've had amniocentesis or chorionic villus sampling, you can't be absolutely sure of your baby's sex until he or she is born. Also, with neutral décor, you avoid teaching your child gender stereotypes and have a room that will suit future children of either sex.
- Keep your baby's development in mind. Here are a few ways to catch your baby's interest:
  - Use mirrors in the nursery. Long before babies realize who's smiling back from the mirror, they love to gaze at their own reflection, fascinated by what they see there. This encourages self-recognition, which enhances emotional development. It also fosters eye-hand coordination as baby reaches to touch the mirror.

- Place something interesting behind the rocking chair and the changing table to give baby a focal point. Mobiles, wind chimes, wall hangings, mirrors, and pictures all work well.
- Use sheets patterned with highly contrasting colors. Infants respond to contrasting colors like black and white.
- Hang sun catchers in the window.

Money-Saving Tips

- If you're purchasing new baby gear, approach a store with several members of your childbirth class and ask for a volume discount.
- Some baby stores give discount coupons to hospitals and clinics. Find out if such coupons are available through your caregiver's office or your birth site.
- Buy multiple-use baby gear, such as:
  - A crib that converts to a juvenile bed
  - A dresser that converts to a changing table
  - A highchair that converts to a juvenile booster chair
  - A carriage that converts to a stroller
- Buy secondhand baby gear from consignment stores, garage sales, newspaper classified ads, social service agencies, preschool newsletters, friends and relatives, community bulletin boards, or Internet sources. When buying used gear, ask the following questions:
  - Who is the manufacturer? (Be sure to register with the manufacturer so your investment will be covered in the event of a recall.)
  - What is the style name or number?
  - Is a manual available?
  - How old is the item?
  - How many children used the item?
  - Is it assembled?
  - Are any parts missing?
  - What's the general condition of the item (including structural integrity, loose items, or worn areas)?
  - Does the item meet safety standards?
- Improve older baby equipment by:
  - Repainting with high-gloss nontoxic paint and making any necessary safety updates.
  - Decorating furniture with decals to coordinate with those on the nursery walls. (Be sure to place decals where they are inaccessible to your baby.)
  - Cutting letters, animals, numbers, and so on from leftover wallpaper and using them to decorate a crib headboard or dresser or to line changing table shelves, bookcase shelves, or drawers.
  - Buying or making covers for worn highchairs, infant seats, play yards, or changing table pads. (King-size pillowcases fit standard-size changing table pads.)

Used Gear Search Notes

Use the following chart to help you investigate baby gear advertised by various sources.

Item	Cost	Source	Phone Number	Address/ Directions

Safety Guidelines

Follow these guidelines to ensure your baby's safety.

General Safety

- Mail all completed product registration and warranty cards so you're notified of manufacturer recalls.
- Check that all new baby gear has a certification safety seal from the Juvenile Products Manufacturers Association (JPMA).
- Don't place any gear directly under ceiling fans or by heating elements or windows.

Crib Safety

- Check that the space between slats is no more than 2⅜ inches wide.
- Make sure there are no missing, loose, cracked, or splintered slats.
- Make sure the crib has no sharp or jagged edges.
- Check that the mattress fits snugly in the crib. (No more than two fingers fit between the edge of the mattress and the side of the crib.)
- Securely attach the mattress support to the headboard and footboard.
- Make sure the screws or bolts holding crib parts together are tight and none are missing.
- Check that corner posts are 1/16 inch high or less.
- Check that the headboard or footboard have no cutouts.
- Make sure the side rail latch is too difficult for a young child to release.
- Check that the top of the side rail, when lowered completely, is at least four inches above the mattress.
- Cover the mattress with a well-fitting crib sheet.
- Don't place any pillows, comforters, stuffed animals, or other soft items in the crib.
- Make sure the hanging items on mobiles aren't long enough to strangle a child.
- Once your child can get on hands and knees, remove crib gyms and hanging mobiles from the crib.

Bassinet or Cradle Safety

- Make sure the bassinet or cradle has a sturdy bottom and a wide, stable base.
- Follow the manufacturer's guidelines on the appropriate weight and size of babies that can use the bassinet or cradle safely.
- Check that the spaces between spindles are no more than 2⅜ inches wide.
- Make sure the screws and bolts are tight.
- Make sure foldable legs have secure locks.

- Check that the mattress is firm and smooth and fits snugly. (No more than two fingers fit between the edge of the mattress and the side of the bassinet or cradle).
- Check that trim and decorative bows and ribbons are stitched securely.
- Make sure there's sufficient wall clearance for swinging or rocking cradles.
- Make sure a swinging or rocking cradle can be immobilized.
- Don't place any pillows, comforters, stuffed animals, or other soft items in the bassinet or cradle.

Changing Area Safety

- Check that the legs of a changing table or dresser are wide and stable. The item shouldn't feel rickety when you shake it.
- Make sure the changing area has a sturdy guardrail (the higher, the better), secure safety straps, and a pad that stays put.
- If the changing area is a fold-out leaf, make sure it can steadily support a baby's weight at the edge farthest from the hinge.
- Check that the changing area has a place to store supplies, and that the storage areas are out of reach of a mobile baby.

Pacifier Safety

- Make sure the pacifier is in one piece and has a soft nipple. (Do not use bottle nipples. Alone, they're too small to be safe. Even when attached to a ring collar, a bottle nipple may be pulled loose by strong sucking.)
- Check that the shield is at least 1½ inches across and is made of firm plastic with air holes.
- Use a pacifier that's dishwasher safe. For babies older than six months, you can wash pacifiers with soap and rinse them in clear water.
- Make sure the pacifier is the right size for your child. (Pacifiers come in two sizes: one for the first six months and the second for older children.)
- Check that the pacifier doesn't have ribbons attached to it. (Tying a pacifier to a crib or to your child poses the risk of strangulation.)
- Replace the pacifier when the rubber has changed color or becomes torn.

Bouncer Seat Safety

- Make sure the seat has secure safety straps.
- Never place your baby in the bouncer seat on an elevated surface like a table. Your baby's bouncing may cause the seat to move, perhaps off the edge of the surface.
- Stop using the seat when your child exceeds the manufacturer's recommended weight and/or development. Your child's movements could tip over the bouncer seat.

Car Seat Safety

- Read the manufacturer's instructions and always keep them with the seat.
- Read your vehicle owner's manual for important information on how to install a car seat correctly in your vehicle.
- Install the car seat in the back seat. Never place a child younger than twelve years old in the front seat of a vehicle.
- Face the child safety seat in the correct direction for the size and age of your child.
- Properly attach the car seat to the vehicle's seat belt or Lower Anchors and Tethers for Children (LATCH) system. (All passenger vehicles and car safety seats made after September 2002 come with the LATCH system. Unless both the vehicle and the car seat have this system, you'll need seat belts to secure the seat.) Check the manufacturer's instructions to route the seat belt or LATCH through the correct path on the car seat. The seat shouldn't move more than an inch side to side or toward the front of the car. Buckle or attach it, and pull it tight.
- If using the seat belt, check the buckle to make sure it doesn't lie just at the point where the belt bends around the car seat. (If it does, you won't get the belt tight enough.) Check your vehicle's manual to see if you can lock the seat belts into position or if you'll need to use a locking clip. Locking clips come with all new car seats. (Some have them built in.) Read the instructions for information on how to use the locking clip.
- Use the correct harness slots for the child's size.
- Place the plastic harness clip, if provided, at armpit level to hold shoulder straps in place.
- Make sure the straps lie flat and aren't twisted. Adjust the straps to accommodate the thickness of your child's clothes, checking that the harness still holds the child snugly.
- If your baby's head slumps forward, the seat may not be reclined enough. Tilt the car seat until it's reclined as close as possible to a forty-five–degree angle (according to manufacturer's instructions).
- Dress your baby in clothes that allow the car seat straps between the legs.
- In cold weather, tuck blankets around your baby *after* securing and adjusting the harness straps. Don't place blankets under your baby.
- Pad the sides and crotch of the seat with rolled-up receiving blankets to keep your newborn from slouching.
- If using built-in car seats, make sure you follow the manufacturer's weight and height recommendations. All built-ins are for children at least a year old and who weigh at least twenty pounds.

- For individual help installing a specific car safety seat in a specific car, consult a certified child passenger safety (CPS) technician. Visit the National Highway Traffic Safety Administration website (http://www.nhtsa.dot.gov) for a list of certified technicians.
- If you're transporting a premature or very small infant, use a car seat without a shield. While still in the hospital, your baby should be observed in the car seat to make sure the semi-reclined position doesn't lower your baby's heart rate or oxygen level or cause other breathing problems.
- Tips for buying or borrowing used car seats:
  - Don't use a seat that's more than ten years old. Check with the manufacturer to find out how long it recommends using the seat. Some manufacturers recommend that consumers use the seats for only five or six years.
  - Don't use a seat if you don't know its entire history. Never use a seat that's been in a crash.
  - Don't use a seat that doesn't have a label stating the manufacture date and seat name or model number.
  - Don't use a seat that doesn't come with manufacturer's instructions.
  - Don't use a seat that has cracks in its frame.
  - Don't use a seat that's missing parts. If you want to use the seat, check first with the manufacturer to make sure you can replace the missing parts.

Fire and Carbon Monoxide (CO) Safety

- Place at least one smoke detector on every floor of your home.
- Place smoke detectors near bedrooms, including the nursery, either on the ceiling or six to twelve inches below the ceiling on the wall.
- Test smoke detectors according to manufacturer's instructions at least once a month, and keep them in working condition at all times.
- Replace batteries according to manufacturer's instructions at least every year.
- Never disconnect the batteries.
- Make sure the detector has a distinct warning signal that you can hear whether you're asleep or awake.
- Use CO detectors that are officially approved by one of the major CO alarm standards: UL2034 (American), EN50291 (European), or BS7860 (British).
- Follow manufacturer's recommendations for placement of CO detectors in your home.
- Test CO detectors at least once a month, following the manufacturer's instructions.
- Replace CO detectors and batteries according to the manufacturer's instructions (usually every five years).

Juvenile Product Safety Information

Consumer Product Safety Commission (CPSC)
Regulates cribs and other baby gear.
Mailing address: U.S. CPSC, Washington, DC 20207-0001
Phone: 800-638-2772
Fax: 301-504-0124 and 301-504-0025
E-mail: info@cpsc.gov
Website: http://www.cpsc.gov

National Highway Traffic Safety Administration (NHTSA)
Regulates and evaluates car seats.
Mailing address: NHTSA, 400 7th St. SW, Washington, DC 20590
Phone: 888-327-4236
E-mail: Send e-mail via online form at http://www.nhtsa.dot.gov/email.cfm.
Website: http://www.nhtsa.dot.gov

Juvenile Products Manufacturers Association (JPMA)
Informs consumers, the industry, and its members about the safe use of juvenile products, industry issues, and the JPMA.
Mailing address: JPMA, 17000 Commerce Pkwy., Suite C, Mt. Laurel, NJ 08054
Phone: 856-638-0420
Fax: 856-439-0525
E-mail: jpma@ahint.com
Website: http://www.jpma.org

Tips for Arranging the Nursery

After you've gathered all the baby gear you need, you must figure out where to put it. Following are some tips to help you plan a safe and functional nursery.

- Determine where your baby will be spending time (for example, bed, changing area, bouncer seat, swing, or play yard) and keep that gear away from anything that may disturb baby (such as bright light or noise from a window), cause baby discomfort (such as a draft from a window, vent, fan, or outside wall), or put baby in danger by creating a fire risk or by tempting baby to grab, pull, chew, poke, or climb (such as a door, window, window treatment, light switch, electrical cord or outlet, shelf, or space heater).
- Place your baby's changing area near his or her dresser (or wherever you'll be storing clothes).

- Place heavy furniture in which your baby won't be spending time (like a dresser) in front of electrical outlets; that way the outlets and the cords plugged into them will be inaccessible to baby once he or she is mobile.
- Allow space for walking, playing, and smooth traffic flow.
- Make the chair where you'll be spending lots of time feeding and cuddling your baby comfortable and pleasant for you by placing it within arm's reach of anything you may want (such as a lamp; a blanket or pillow; a radio or CD player; a shelf, table, or container to hold a snack, water bottle, reading material, cordless phone, and so on).
- Allow ample clearance from walls and electrical cords for moving items like rocking chairs, cradles, swings, and rotating mobiles.

Chapter Five

Family and Household Needs

Life with a newborn is hectic. Life with a newborn and an older child can be even more chaotic. This chapter is designed to help your whole family get ready for its newest member. You'll find helpful hints on when to tell your older child about the baby, suggestions to help make the transition easier for everyone, and ideas for organizing your household so *everyone* has time to relax.

Sibling Planning

Timing Your Announcement

Consider your child's age, development, and emotional maturity as you decide when and how to tell him or her about your new baby. Following are some strategic moments that may be right for your child.

- When your child expresses fear that Mommy is sick, or your child seems sensitive to any vomiting, faintness, mood swings, or other symptoms you may be having.
- When your pregnancy begins to show, and/or your child begins to wonder why Mommy is getting fat.
- When there's a chance that another person may tell your child before you do.
- After the first trimester, when the risk of a miscarriage decreases.
- After your child has adjusted to any of the following major changes:
  - Weaning
  - Potty training
  - Moving into a bed from a crib
  - Moving into another bedroom
  - Moving into a booster seat from a highchair
  - Moving into a new car seat
  - Enrolling in a nursery school or playgroup
  - Moving to a new home

Preparing Your Child for Baby

- To make the waiting period understandable, link your baby's arrival with a season rather than a month.
- Attend a sibling preparation class and hospital tour with your child.
- Bring your child to a prenatal checkup so s/he can meet your caregiver.

- Give your child a realistic idea of what to expect in the first few weeks after the baby's birth: You'll be tired, the baby will take lots of your time, and the baby will not be able to do much. Visit friends with a new baby, if possible.
- Read books about pregnancy, birth, newborns, and baby siblings with your child. Give him or her a chance to ask questions, voice concerns, and vent feelings inspired by the books.
- Look at pictures and/or watch videos of your child's birth and babyhood. Tell your child about the birth, what s/he was like as a baby, how excited you were, and how everyone wanted to see and hold him or her.
- Have your child practice holding a doll and supporting the head. Teach him or her how to touch and hold a baby very gently.
- Let your child participate in baby preparations if s/he is interested.
- Consider having your child present at the baby's birth if it seems right for your family.
- Tell your child beforehand who will take care of him or her while you're giving birth.

Helping Your Child Adjust to Baby

- Introduce your child to the baby as soon as possible, preferably with no other visitors present. Have the children exchange gifts. Share a birthday cake to celebrate the baby's birth and to help your child understand why the baby is getting so many gifts.
- Change your child's routine as little as possible.
- Spend (and see that your partner spends) some uninterrupted one-on-one time with your child every day.
- Listen carefully to your child's feelings about the baby and the changes in your family. Help your child put his or her feelings into words if necessary. Acknowledge negative feelings—never deny or discount them.
- Make sure your child understands that absolutely no hurting is allowed. Give your child safe ways to express negative feelings, like drawing angry pictures, acting out with dolls, or roaring like a lion.
- Baby your child if s/he seems to need it. Don't worry about regression, which is likely to be short-lived. Expect less independence, and you're likely to get more.
- Have some special gifts to give your child when friends and relatives show up with baby gifts, so your older child won't feel left out.
- Remind visitors to pay attention to your older child as well as the baby and encourage them to discuss topics other than what it's like to have a baby sister or brother.

- Make sure your child has some private space and things that he or she doesn't have to share with the baby.
- Give your child special jobs to help the family and the baby, but don't overdo it—take your cues from your child.
- Point out the benefits of being an older child, like choosing what to eat, being able to go the park and play, and having friends.
- Plan ahead for times when your baby will need your full attention, such as feedings and colicky times. Write out a list of quiet activities to suggest to your older child, such as:
  - Reading stories
  - Listening to music or audiobooks
  - Coloring or drawing
  - Watching a high-quality TV program or video
  - Playing a favorite game
  - Playing with a special toy reserved for such times
  - Nurturing a doll in the same way you're nurturing the baby

Household Management

At the very time when you least want to think about housework—and have little energy to do it—a disorganized household can overwhelm you. The best way to reduce stress in this area is to lower your expectations. Remember that you just can't do it all, and that caring for your baby, yourself, and the rest of your family is more important than having a spotless home. Another useful strategy: Analyze your household needs before your baby's birth and plan ahead to meet those needs. Putting a system in place can prevent arguments, keep your household running smoothly, and save you from managing all the details.

Duty Roster

Do you have a housekeeping pet peeve? Perhaps it's dirty dishes in the sink or newspapers strewn about the living room. Little peeves can become big problems during postpartum, when everyone's exhausted. Defuse emotional time bombs with planning. Accept offers of help from friends and relatives. Hire a neighborhood kid to mow the lawn or weed the garden. Distribute duties like those on the following list among family members and helpers.

Chore	Frequency	Person Responsible
Do laundry		
Take out garbage		
Wash dishes		
Shop for groceries		
Prepare dinner		
Pay bills		
Run errands		
Dust furniture		
Pick up newspapers/mail		
Clean bathroom		
Sweep floors		
Vacuum floors		
Wash floors		
Clean mirrors		
Pick up clothes		
Mow lawn		
Shovel snow		
Weed garden		
Fuel vehicles		
Wash vehicles		
Other:		

Household Schedule

The first month postpartum is likely to be a whirlwind. To help you remember activities, events, and tasks you have scheduled, look over the following list and jot your family's schedule on the postpartum calendar on the next page. Be sure to include times and locations. (A map might also be handy for out-of-town helpers.) Post the calendar in a central location in your home.

- Sports practices
- Lessons and classes (music, dance, language, religious, exercise, and so on)
- School hours
- Carpooling
- Events for which you have tickets (sports, arts, and so on)
- Meetings (club, committee, parent-teacher, work-related, and so on)
- Parties
- Special events
- Religious services
- Pet feeding and walking
- Garbage pickup
- Deliveries (mail, groceries, and so on)

Sunday				
Monday				
Tuesday				
Wednesday				
Thursday				
Friday				
Saturday				

Shopping Organizer

Household Supplies

Well before your due date, check out the following list and stock up on the items you use so you'll be prepared for the busy, messy days to come.

Laundry

- Laundry detergent (A perfume-, dye-, and bleach-free detergent should work well for everyone's clothes and skin, including baby's.)
- Prewash and spot remover
- Bleach
- Hydrogen peroxide
- Vinegar
- Cream of tartar
- Borax
- Baking soda
- Lemon juice
- Ammonia
- Fabric softener
- Clothespins

Cleanup

- Floor cleaner and wax
- Furniture polish
- Glass cleaner
- Bathroom cleaner
- Dishwashing liquid
- Dishwasher soap
- Bleach
- Club soda
- Cornstarch
- Vinegar
- Salt
- Lemon juice
- Olive, vegetable, lemon, or linseed oil
- Baking soda
- Borax
- Rubbing alcohol
- Ammonia
- Cream of tartar

Paper and Plastic Products

- Toilet paper
- Facial tissues
- Paper towels
- Garbage bags
- Disposable plates, cups, eating utensils, and baking dishes
- Paper napkins
- Food wrap and storage containers for leftovers

Groceries

Maintain a two-week supply of staples for your family and visitors. Consider stocking up on the following items:

In the Cupboard

- ◇ Canned tomatoes, tomato sauce, tomato paste
- ◇ Jarred spaghetti sauce
- ◇ Canned beans
- ◇ Canned tuna, salmon
- ◇ Rice and pasta
- ◇ Cereal
- ◇ Dried fruit
- ◇ Graham crackers, pretzels, popcorn
- ◇ Flour and sugar
- ◇ Oil and vinegar
- ◇ Miscellaneous spices
- ◇ Pet food

In the Freezer

- ◇ Frozen juices
- ◇ Frozen waffles
- ◇ Frozen vegetables
- ◇ Chicken, turkey breast
- ◇ Trout, salmon, sole, shrimp
- ◇ Lean hamburger
- ◇ Lean frozen entrées

In the Refrigerator

- ◇ Fresh fruits and vegetables
- ◇ Milk
- ◇ Eggs
- ◇ Cheeses
- ◇ Yogurt
- ◇ Butter and/or spreads
- ◇ Deli meats
- ◇ Peanut butter and jam or jelly
- ◇ Mayonnaise, sour cream, and salad dressing

Quick, No-Cook Meal Tips

- Save takeout restaurant coupons, especially from restaurants that are on your family's daily travel route.
- Collect menus from favorite restaurants that deliver.
- During the last weeks of your pregnancy, double any one-dish meals (casseroles, soups, stir-fries, and so on) you make and freeze the extras.
- Accept food contributions from friends or arrange for a meal shower. Usually a friend will plan this event for a family with a new baby. When the baby's born, the friend solicits friends and relatives of the family to deliver home-cooked meals at regular intervals.
- Keep an eye on the specials at your local deli.

Coupons

Postpartum is the ideal time to use coupons. After your baby's birth you'll be continually buying baby supplies, and your consumption of food and other household supplies is likely to rise. Clipping coupons can save you money and make shopping easier for helpers who may not be familiar with the products you want. All the shopper has to do is find the item that matches the coupon. Using coupons at discount stores and/or buying clubs saves even more money.

You can find a slew of coupons on the Internet. Use the keywords *coupons* and *online* to find websites that feature online coupons you can print and redeem at any retailer that carries the product or at a specific retailer. Some online coupons are valid for Internet orders only. Friends, family, and coworkers can also help you collect coupons. Following are a couple of sample notices that can be left with envelopes in workplace community areas, such as lounges, bulletin boards, or cafeterias.

- "I work in (department) and am having a baby in (month). If you come across any coupons for baby supplies that you don't need yourself, I'd greatly appreciate it if you'd pass them along to me. Thanks for your help! (name)"
- My (daughter/sister/friend/niece/granddaughter) is having a baby in (month). Being a practical future (grandpa/aunt/whatever), I'm collecting coupons for baby supplies. If you find any such coupons that you don't need yourself, please donate them to the cause. Thanks for your help! (name)"

Chapter Six

Financial Planning

Examining Your Budget

Unless you're independently wealthy, adding a new family member is bound to stretch your budget. Additional expenditures for healthcare and baby gear often combine with the cost of caring for your baby (loss of income or daycare fees) to create a tight financial situation. The following worksheet will help you examine the impact of a new baby on your budget and identify the childcare scenario(s) that may work for you. (See Chapter Eight for tools to help you choose appropriate childcare.)

How to Use the Worksheet

1. Start with the columns labeled "Earner 1," "Earner 2," and "2-Earner Totals" in the income section. Your most recent paycheck stubs should provide the current wage and deduction information you need for each earner. To determine annual wages and deductions, multiply the amount per pay stub in each category by the number of paychecks received each year (twelve if paid once a month, twenty-four if paid twice a month, or twenty-six if paid every two weeks). Now enter any interest, dividends, or capital gains distributions you earn. Finally, enter any other income you receive, such as rent from rental properties, royalties, or freelance income. To determine your total net income, add your net wages, savings and investment income, and other income.
2. Now fill in the same three columns in the expenses section. Some expenses are work-related while some aren't; some are relatively constant while others may change from month to month. You may have nothing to enter in some categories or may need to add categories that aren't included in the worksheet. Record your current expenses as realistically as possible. This is easy if you've been using a computer program to track expenditures from your checking account. But even if you haven't, you can still gather data about your expenses fairly easily. If you pay for most things by check or debit card, mine your checking account register and/or bank statement for the information you need. For expenses you cover with cash, save receipts for at least a month. Multiply your monthly total or monthly average in each category by twelve to get an annual amount. To determine your total expenses, simply add up all the expenses you've listed.
3. To determine your current cash flow, subtract your total two-earner expenses from your total two-earner net income. If you're following a workable household budget, your current cash flow will be either zero or a positive number.
4. In the column labeled "Changes," enter additions and subtractions to your income and expenses that you expect to make. For example, if you

plan to quit your job, enter your net wages as a negative number. This change might put your family in a lower tax bracket. If so, your partner's tax withholding might drop, thereby increasing his or her net wages. Enter that increase as a positive number. If you decide to get rid of your cable TV subscription, enter your annual cable cost as a negative number. If you think your heating bill might go up because you won't turn down your thermostat daily as you do with both parents working outside the home, enter the estimated annual increase as a positive number. If you like, jot an explanatory note beside each change. To compare different scenarios (for example, one full-time and one part-time earner, two part-time earners, or one full-time earner), photocopy the worksheet and adjust the "Changes" column accordingly for each scenario.

5. Add or subtract the amounts in the "Changes" column from those in the "2-Earner Totals" column to determine your "Revised Totals."
6. To determine your revised cash flow, subtract your revised total expenses from your revised net income. Your goal, of course, is either positive or zero cash flow. You may need to adjust the figures in the "Changes" column to achieve this goal.

Financial Planning Worksheet

	Earner 1	Earner 2	2-Earner Totals	Changes (+ additions, - subtractions)	Revised Totals
ANNUAL INCOME					
Wages					
Gross wages					
Deduction: pretax insurance					
Deduction: pretax medical expenses					
Deduction: pretax dependent care					
Deduction: state income tax					
Deduction: federal income tax					
Deduction: other withholdings					
Deduction: pretax retirement plan contributions					
Net wages (gross wages minus deductions)					
Savings and Investment Income					
Capital gain distributions					
Interest and dividends					
Other Income					
Net business income					
Net rental income					
Net miscellaneous income					
Total Net Income (wages plus other income)					

	Earner 1	Earner 2	2-Earner Totals	Changes (+ additions, - subtractions)	Revised Totals
ANNUAL EXPENSES					
Housing					
Rent					
Mortgage (principal plus interest)					
Homeowner's insurance					
Real estate taxes					
Personal property taxes					
Water					
Trash removal					
Natural gas					
Electricity					
Telephone					
Cable					
Internet					
Landscaping and gardening					
Maintenance					
New furniture					
New appliances					
Transportation					
Car payment					
New car fund (savings)					
Fuel					
Maintenance					
Insurance					
Parking					
Bus fare					
Food					
Groceries and liquor					
Family dining out					
Workday lunches, coffee breaks, and happy hours out					
Medical Expenses					
After-tax insurance costs					
After-tax out-of-pocket costs					
Child-Related Expenses					
After-tax daycare costs					
Tuition					
Diapers and formula					
Uniforms					
Allowance					

	Earner 1	Earner 2	2-Earner Totals	Changes (+ additions, - subtractions)	Revised Totals
Clothing and Personal Care					
Work-related clothing and clothing care					
Hair and skin care					
Other clothing and personal care (all family members)					
Entertainment					
Movies, theater, concerts, CDs					
Date nights					
Babysitters					
Holidays					
Gifts					
Travel					
Entertaining					
Decorating					
Gifts					
Charitable contributions					
Wedding and baby showers					
Birthdays					
Other gifts					
Recreation and Hobbies					
Memberships (museum, health club, zoo, and so on)					
Fees for children's lessons, teams, and clubs					
Adult recreation fees					
Supplies and equipment					
Toys and games					
Computers and other electronics					
Vacation					
Transportation					
Lodging					
Entertainment and activities					
Food					
Pet boarding					
Pet Care					
Veterinarian					
Food					
Supplies					

	Earner 1	Earner 2	2-Earner Totals	Changes (+ additions, - subtractions)	Revised Totals
Savings and Investment Expenses					
Emergency savings					
After-tax retirement plan contributions					
College savings					
Stocks					
Other investments					
Miscellaneous Expenses					
Household sundries					
Postage					
Office contributions					
Professional associations					
Subscriptions					
Spending money					
Total Expenses					
CASH FLOW (+ surplus, - deficit)					

Income

If you've used the preceding Financial Planning Worksheet, you probably have a good idea of how much income you'll need to support your family. Now you need to decide how you'll make that income.

Work-Family Scenarios

When parental leave ends, many parents return to business as usual. Many others change their employment status. Following are a few scenarios you might consider if you're a two-parent family:

- Both parents earn income full-time.
- One parent earns full-time; one earns part-time.
- Both parents earn part-time.
- One parent earns full-time; one cares for the child(ren) full-time.

Flexible Employment

Some parents balance childcare and household management with income-producing work by staggering their schedules or working at home or part-time. Here are some flexible employment options you may want to investigate:

- Sharing a full-time job with another employee (job-sharing)
- Working at a job that's designed to be part-time
- Working weekends, nights, and/or evenings
- Working flexible hours (according to your employer's and family's needs)
- Working a compressed workweek
- Seasonal work
- Substitute or backup employment
- Working odd jobs
- Working someplace where your child can accompany you
- Working at home

Working at Home

Here are some types of work that can be done easily at home or using home as a base of operations:

- Freelancing (writing, editing, illustration, marketing, graphic design, performing arts, tutoring, giving lessons, modeling, professional coaching, catering)
- Telephone- and computer-based jobs (programming, research, medical transcription, customer service, credit card payment processing)
- Telecommuting (keeping your pre-baby job but doing it at home)
- Direct sales (selling a specific line of products, such as cosmetics, kitchen products, party supplies, clothing, candles, baskets, craft supplies, and so on)
- Personal services (hair stylists, accountants, tarot readers)
- Home child care or elder care
- Piecework (sewing, baking, assembling)
- Landlord or caretaker

Working at home may suit you if:

1. You're self-motivated and self-disciplined.
2. You're enthusiastic and tenacious.
3. You have a good attention span and ability to focus.
4. You manage your time and space well.
5. You know how much time you can realistically commit.
6. You know how you'll balance the demands of work and family while you're at home.
7. You can cope well under stress.
8. Your family supports you.
9. You have the equipment and space for a home office.
10. You have an aptitude for learning new things.
11. You try to improve and educate yourself continually.

12. You can offer a high-quality product or service at a price people will pay that will make a profit for you.
13. You're prepared to handle all three main functions of a business (selling, producing, and administrating).
14. You can clearly articulate who'll buy from you, how you'll make them aware of you, why they should buy from you and not your competitors, and how you'll deliver your goods or services.

If you choose to work at home:

- Designate a room or part of a room in your home as your office. Set up a desk, computer, phone, and so on, and store your supplies and records in this space. Use it as a home base for your work.
- Obtain a cordless phone or a phone headset. Make sure the phone has a "mute" button.
- Consider ordering an extra phone line with a separate number and a custom ring that alerts you to business calls. You can instruct family members not to answer your work phone or custom ring—or at least to greet business callers politely.
- Be prepared to switch gears. You'll either have to ignore the noises outside your office, trusting that your childcare provider or partner is handling things just fine, or you'll have to juggle your professional and parental roles depending on who needs you more at any given moment.
- Set aside a small space in your office where your child can play quietly.

Back-to-Work Checklist

If you or your partner is planning to return to (or begin) a job after having a baby, you may need to do the following:

- Investigate company policy and attitudes, as well as your legal rights, regarding parental leave (for example, to care for a sick child or attend parent-teacher conferences)
- Investigate company policy and attitudes, as well as your legal rights, regarding breastfeeding. Make arrangements for expressing milk during the workday, including break time; privacy; a pump, collection kit, and storage supplies; and a safe storage place for milk.
- Add your baby as participant in employer-sponsored insurance plan(s).
- Adjust flexible spending paycheck deductions.
- Add your baby as a beneficiary of your retirement savings or life insurance plan.
- Arrange for primary and backup childcare. (See Chapter Eight.)
- Reserve paid time off for use if a family emergency occurs.
- Adjust your baby's daily routine to accommodate a new schedule.

Insurance

Pregnancy is the perfect time to get all your insurance records in order and questions answered. The following charts will help you organize this information.

Insurance Information

Insurance Company

Name: ____
Mailing address for claims: ____________________________
Customer service phone number: ________________________
Precertification phone number: _________________________
Nurse line: ____
Insurance agent's name and phone number: __________________

Policy

Member name: _____________________________________
Member identification number: _________________________
Policy, account, or group number: _______________________
Policy effective dates: ________________________________

Deductibles

Family: ____
Individual: _______________________________________
For mother: ______________________________________
For baby: ____
Can costs incurred during the last three months of the year be carried over into the new year's deductible? __________________________

Coverage

Evaluate your health insurance coverage and plan for your maternity costs by using the following checklist. Avoid unnecessary costs by learning what your insurance policy will and will not cover, and learn how to submit bills and request services in the language of your insurance policy.

Individual who answered my questions: ______________________
Date: ____
Verified by attached correspondence dated: ___________________

General

Does the policy have any preexisting condition limitations? ____________

____

How do I add my baby to my policy? ______________________________
When does coverage begin for my newborn? ________________________
Does my baby's health at birth affect newborn care coverage? ________

____

Is preapproval required for any tests, procedures, or medications? ______
If so, which ones? _______________________________________

____

How is preapproval obtained? _____________________________
Does the policy allow me to select my physician and hospital, or must I use only those affiliated with my health maintenance organization (HMO)?

____

____

Is there a "reasonable and customary" clause in the policy? ___________
(This means that the policy will cover only fees that are considered average for your community.)
What's the procedure for submitting claims? ______________________

____

How is payment made? _______________________________________

Item	Percentage	Conditions
Maternal Care		
Services		
Caregiver fees		
Obstetrical caregivers		
Ob-gyn		
Perinatologist		
Reproductive endocrinologist		
Family physician		
General practitioner		
Certified nurse-midwife		
Women's health nurse practitioner		
Certified midwife		
Certified professional midwife		
Direct-entry midwife		
Lay midwife		
Naturopathic doctor		

Item	Percentage	Conditions
Obstetrical care		
Infertility treatments		
Prenatal checkups		
Vaginal delivery		
Cesarean delivery		
Hospital visits		
Phone consultations		
Postpartum checkup		
Other caregivers		
Anesthesiologist		
Doula		
Lactation consultant		
Genetic counselor		
Dentist		
Nursing care		
Private		
Staff		
Home		
Classes		
Childbirth		
Exercise		
Nutrition		
Breastfeeding		
First aid		
Baby care		
Medication		
Outpatient		
Prescribed		
Administered		
Inpatient		
Prescribed		
Administered		
Anesthetic		
General		
Regional and local		
Epidural		
Spinal		
Sterile water block		
Pudendal block		
Paracervical block		
Perineal block		
Intravenous (IV) fluids		

Item	Percentage	Conditions
Supplies		
Sanitary pads		
Breast pump and collection kit		
Nursing pads		
Lanolin cream		
Sitz bath		
Cleansing bottle		
Witch hazel pads		
"Doughnut" pillow		
Procedures		
Urine test to detect:		
Pregnancy		
Urinary tract bacteria		
Sugar		
Ketones		
Protein		
Blood test to detect:		
Pregnancy		
Blood type		
Rh factor or Rh antibodies		
Anemia		
Infectious organisms or antibodies against them		
Blood glucose levels		
Genetic disorder(s)		
Toxoplasmosis		
Multiple marker screening		
Group B streptococcus screening		
Amniocentesis		
Biophysical profile		
Chorionic villus sampling		
Contraction stress test or oxytocin challenge test		
Cordocentesis or percutaneous umbilical blood sampling		
Doppler blood flow study		
Glucose tolerance test		
Magnetic resonance imaging		
Non-stress test		
Ultrasound (sonography)		
Vaginal/cervical smear		
X-ray		

Item	Percentage	Conditions
Newborn Care		
Caregiver Fees		
Pediatric caregivers		
Pediatrician		
Neonatologist		
Family physician		
General practitioner		
Pediatric or family nurse practitioner		
Physician's assistant		
Naturopath or other alternative practitioner		
Pediatric care		
Initial interview		
Inpatient visits		
Routine newborn procedures (blood tests, eye treatment, and so on)		
Outpatient visits		
Well-baby		
Sick-baby		
Vaccinations		
Nursery Supplies		
Cap(s)		
Receiving blanket(s)		
T-shirts		
Diapers		
Bottles		
Formula		
Medication		
Surgical supplies		
Incubators		
Oxygen		
IV		
Monitors		
Bilirubin lights		

Item	Percentage	Conditions
Hospital Costs		
Rooms		
Emergency room		
Labor room		
Birthing room		
Operating room		
Recovery room		
Postpartum room		
Private		
Semiprivate		
Telephone		
Television		
Board		
Patient's meals		
Guest trays		

Baby's Future

It's never too soon to make arrangements for your baby's future. Organizing and recording your family legal and financial information, as well as saving and investing on your baby's behalf, can lead to a more secure future for your child.

Legal and Financial Professionals

Attorney

Name: ______________________________
Address: ______________________________
Phone: ______________________________
Fax: ______________________________
E-mail: ______________________________
Location of important papers (like wills): ______________________________
____
____

Accountant

Name: ____
Address: ____
Phone: ____
Fax: ____
E-mail: ____
Location of important papers (like tax returns): ____________
____
____

Investment Broker

Name: ____
Address: ____
Phone: ____
Fax: ____
E-mail: ____
Location of important papers (like stock certificates): ________
____
____

Estate Planner

Name: ____
Address: ____
Phone: ____
Fax: ____
E-mail: ____
Executor of your estate: ____________________________

Financial Advisor

Name: ____
Address: ____
Phone: ____
Fax: ____
E-mail: ____

Insurance Agent

Name: ______________________________
Address: ______________________________
Phone: ______________________________
Fax: ______________________________
E-mail: ______________________________
Location of important papers (like policies): ______________________________

____

____

Parents' Fact Sheet

Complete this form and keep it in a safe place. This information might be necessary at a later date when your child applies for a passport, benefits, and so on. If you've died, the information might not be easily accessible to your child's guardian.

Information

Mother
Full name: ______________________________
Date of birth: ______________________________
Place of birth: ______________________________
City: ______________________________
County: ______________________________
State (or country): ______________________________
Social security number: ______________________________
Full name of mother (baby's grandmother): ______________________________
Date of birth: ______________________________
Place of birth: ______________________________
Full name of father (baby's grandfather): ______________________________
Date of birth: ______________________________
Place of birth: ______________________________

Father
Full name: ______________________________
Date of birth: ______________________________
Place of birth: ______________________________
City: ______________________________
County: ______________________________
State (or country): ______________________________
Social security number: ______________________________

Full name of mother (baby's grandmother): ____________________

Date of birth: ____________________

Place of birth: ____________________

Full name of father (baby's grandfather): ____________________

Date of birth: ____________________

Place of birth: ____________________

Past Employment

Name of company: ____________________

Address: ____________________

Period of employment: ____________________

Name of company: ____________________

Address: ____________________

Period of employment: ____________________

Name of company: ____________________

Address: ____________________

Period of employment: ____________________

Insurance Policies

Health insurance company: ____________________

Health insurance policy number: ____________________

Life insurance company: ____________________

Life insurance policy number: ____________________

Auto insurance company: ____________________

Auto insurance policy number: ____________________

Homeowner's insurance company: ____________________

Homeowner's insurance policy number: ____________________

Other insurance companies and numbers: ____________________

____

____

____

____

____

Bank Accounts

Institution: ____________________

Type of account: ____________________

Account number: ____________________

Institution: ____________________

Type of account: ____________________

Account number: ____________________

Institution: ____________________

Type of account: ____________________

Account number: ____________________

Retirement Savings

Name of company: ______________________________

Address: ______________________________

Account number: ______________________________

Name of company: ______________________________

Address: ______________________________

Account number: ______________________________

Name of company: ______________________________

Address: ______________________________

Account number: ______________________________

Name of company: ______________________________

Address: ______________________________

Account number: ______________________________

Investments

Type of investment: ______________________________

Name of company: ______________________________

Address: ______________________________

Account number: ______________________________

Type of investment: ______________________________

Name of company: ______________________________

Address: ______________________________

Account number: ______________________________

Type of investment: ______________________________

Name of company: ______________________________

Address: ______________________________

Account number: ______________________________

Family Heirlooms

Type of heirloom: ______________________________

Location: ______________________________

Significance: ______________________________

Approximate value: ______________________________

Type of heirloom: ______________________________

Location: ______________________________

Significance: ______________________________

Approximate value: ______________________________

Type of heirloom: ______________________________

Location: ______________________________

Significance: ______________________________

Approximate value: ______________________________

Personal identification numbers (PINs), passwords, or security codes not recorded elsewhere: ______________________________

____

____

Baby's Social Security Number

The easiest way to apply for your baby's social security number (SSN) is at the hospital. Have both parents' SSNs handy when you do. When the hospital asks you for the information needed to complete your baby's birth certificate, mention that you want to have an SSN assigned to your baby. As part of your state's birth registration process, the state vital statistics office will send to the Social Security Administration (SSA) the information needed to assign your baby a number. Your baby's card will be sent to you in the mail in approximately two weeks.

If you don't apply for the card at the hospital and want to apply at one of the SSA offices, you'll need to fill out an application; show at least two documents as evidence of your child's age, identity, and citizenship; and show evidence of your identity. Following is a list of documents that may be accepted as evidence. All documents must be either originals or copies certified by the issuing agency. The SSA does not accept photocopies or notarized copies.

Child's Age

- Birth certificate (preferred)
- Religious record of birth recorded before three months of age

Child's Identity

- Doctor, clinic, or hospital record
- Religious record (for example, baptismal record)
- Daycare center or school record
- Adoption record
- School ID card

Child's Citizenship

- Birth certificate
- Other document showing U.S. place of birth

Parent's Identity

- Driver's license
- Employer ID card
- Passport
- Marriage or divorce record
- Health insurance card (not a Medicare card)
- Military record
- Life insurance policy
- School ID card

To find your local SSA office, visit http://www.socialsecurity.gov/locator. To download the SSN application form (form SS-5), visit http://www.social security.gov/online/ss-5.html.

Baby's Investments

Record all securities, investments, and/or savings accounts purchased or opened for your child. Such a record is especially helpful in tracking and computing tax liability for long-term investments.

Security	Purchase Price	Number of Shares	Date Purchased

Institution	Type of Account	Account Number

Chapter Seven

Celebrations

Baby Showers

You won't plan your own baby shower, of course, but your input is important so the host knows what day is best, whom to invite, and what you really need. If you have more than one shower, make extra copies of these pages.

Shower Planner

Host: ______________________________

Date: ______________________________

Time: ______________________________

Location: ______________________________

Activity suggestions (if having activities): ______________________________

____

____

____

Menu suggestions: ______________________________

____

____

____

Setting a shower date can be tricky. First you must decide if you want the shower before or after the baby is born. Each has its advantages: Having the shower before means you'll be stocked with baby-related items when your little one arrives. It may also boost your spirits during those last weeks of pregnancy. Having the shower after the birth means the guests can meet the baby and buy sex-specific gifts (if you didn't know or announce the baby's sex before the birth). It also gives you a chance to determine exactly what you need (and don't need) to care for your baby.

If you decide to have the shower before the baby is born, set the date at least four to six weeks before your due date. If you decide to have the shower after the birth, set the date for at least one month after your due date or wait until the baby is born to pick the date. Whenever you have the shower, check the calendar so the date doesn't conflict with a holiday or other special event, such as a family wedding.

Shower Guest List

Name	Address	Phone	RSVP

Before selecting the guest list, discuss with the host whether you want to invite women only or men as well. In years past, only women attended showers. Today, coed showers are becoming more popular. They're a great way to welcome both the mom- and dad-to-be into parenthood.

Assembling the guest list can be difficult. Be sure to talk with the host to narrow your focus. Is this a shower for family (yours and/or your partner's), friends, coworkers, neighbors, members of a place of worship or club, or some combination? Once you decide this, you may find the guest list easy to assemble.

Be sure the size of the guest list doesn't exceed the space and resources available. Consider everything from seating limitations to your host's budget. You may discover you need to trim the list, move the location, or scale back the shower.

Shower Gift List

Fill out this gift list in addition to or in lieu of a gift registry at a department or discount store. Have the host make copies and include them with the shower invitations.

Layette

Quantity	Item	Description
	Disposable diapers	
	Cloth diapers	
	Diaper covers	
	Diaper fasteners	
	Baby wipes	
	Onesies	
	Socks or booties	
	Soft cotton shirts	
	Stretchies or coveralls	
	Sleepers or pajamas	
	Bibs	
	Caps or bonnets	
	Sweaters or jackets	
	Snowsuit or bunting	
	Receiving blankets	
	Warmer blankets	
	Lightweight crib blankets	
	Fitted crib sheets	
	Waterproof mattress pads	
	Waterproof lap pads	
	Washcloths	
	Hand towels	
	Hooded bath towels	
	Burp cloths	
	Other:	

Nursery

Quantity	Item	Description
	Crib	
	Bassinet or cradle	
	Bedside co-sleeper or compact infant bed	
	Changing table	
	Changing pad	
	Dresser	
	Diaper bag	
	Diaper pail	
	Décor items (curtains, wallpaper border, etc.)	
	Play yard	
	Mobile	
	Bouncer seat	
	Swing	
	Rocker, glider, or armchair	
	Lamp	
	Night-light	
	Other:	

Feeding and Bathing

Quantity	Item	Description
	Breast pump	
	Breast milk collection kit	
	Storage bottles or bags	
	Nursing bras	
	Nursing pads	
	Bottles and nipples	
	Bottle brush	
	Bottle sterilizer	
	Portable bottle warmer	
	Nursing pillows	
	Highchair	

Feeding and Bathing (continued)

Quantity	Item	Description
	Baby tub or sink liner	
	Bath thermometer	
	Bath toys	
	Other:	

Health and Safety

Quantity	Item	Description
	Digital thermometer (rectal, ear, or axillary)	
	Cool-mist vaporizer	
	Grooming set (brush/comb)	
	Pacifiers	
	Blunt-edged nail scissors, baby nail clippers, or emery boards	
	Baby soap, lotion, shampoo, and oil	
	Nasal aspirator	
	Medicine dispenser	
	Smoke detectors	
	CO detectors	
	Baby gates	
	Other:	

Electronics

Quantity	Item	Description
	Cell phone	
	Cordless phone	
	Phone services (answering machine, voice mail, caller ID, etc.)	
	Analog or digital camcorder	
	Conventional or digital camera	
	Clock radio	
	Intercom, baby monitor, or walkie-talkies	
	Tape or digital recorder	
	Other:	

Traveling

Quantity	Item	Description
	Stroller	
	Front carrier or sling	
	Backpack (for older babies)	
	Car seat	
	Sunshades for car windows	
	Back-seat mirror (so driver can see a rear-facing baby's face)	
	Other:	

Toys and Keepsakes

Quantity	Item	Description
	Baby book	
	First-year calendar	
	Baby name book	
	Photo frames	
	Plush animals	
	Rattles	
	Cloth books	
	Balls	
	Activity centers	
	Musical toys	
	Stacking or sorting toys	
	Other:	

Books for Parents' Library

Title	Author

Services as Gifts

Description	Details
Watching siblings	
Preparing or delivering meals	
Shopping or running errands	
Cleaning the house	
Doing laundry	
Inviting the new family for dinner	
Making a craft or sewing project	
Starting a savings account for baby	
Assembling baby furniture or equipment	
Painting or wallpapering the nursery	
Helping organize a religious ceremony	

To help guests coordinate gifts, provide information such as the sex of the baby (if known and announced) and the color or theme of your nursery.

Because you'll probably have several big-ticket items on your list, have the shower host encourage guests to buy group gifts or give gift certificates to one specific store.

Special Ceremonies

Many parents celebrate the birth of a baby with a special ceremony or ritual, such as a baptism or christening, bris, blessing, welcoming, or naming ceremony. This is often a time when family and friends gather. It's best to organize the event now, because once your bundle of joy arrives, you'll have little time and energy to spare.

Planning a Special Ceremony

You may wish to customize a ceremony (religious or nonreligious) of your own. If you wish to have a religious ceremony through your place of worship, however, here are some guidelines.

- Contact the officiant at your place of worship to determine the following things:
  - When will the ceremony be held? (You may be able to choose the date, or it may be a specific number of days after the birth.)
  - Where will the ceremony be conducted (at the place of worship, at your home, etc.)?
  - What is the maximum number of guests?
  - What are your family's obligations to the place of worship?
  - Can you customize the ceremony (such as request music, readings, vocalists, celebrants)?
  - Are there requirements for choosing godparents, sponsors, or witnesses?
- Keeping in mind the requirements outlined by your place of worship, choose godparents, sponsors, or witnesses. If they accept the honor, inform them of their obligations and role in the ceremony, if any.
- Decide if you want to dress the baby in a special outfit for the ceremony. If purchasing a new outfit, wait until after the baby is born, unless you know the sex beforehand. If you'd like to use an heirloom outfit, be sure it fits and is in good condition.

Planning a Party to Follow the Ceremony

Whether you have a formal ceremony at your place of worship or a custom ceremony at home, it's a wonderful opportunity to welcome your baby into a community of faith, family, or friends. For this reason, you may enjoy having a party or a get-together following the ceremony. Again, it's best to organize this event before the baby arrives. Here's a checklist to help you do just that.

- Enlist the help of at least one friend or family member. You'll have your hands full with a newborn the day of the celebration, so you'll find it much easier if someone else can execute your plans.
- Select the location and, if necessary, enlist your helper(s) to clean before the party; set up tables, supplies, and food; and clean up after the party.
  - ◇ Community hall at your place of worship
  - ◇ Your home
  - ◇ Other area ______________________________

> Make a guest list, keeping the location's space limitations in mind.

Name	Address	Phone	RSVP*

*Direct RSVPs to your helper(s). When you're home with your newborn, you'll want to keep phone calls and distractions to a minimum.

> Select and preaddress the invitations; once you know the date of the ceremony, send them. Or plan to phone the guests once you know the date.

> Select a menu.

- Cake and punch
- Snack trays (cheese and crackers, vegetables, fruits, hot/cold hors d'oeuvres)
- Meal
  - Prepared and frozen ahead of time
  - Prepared and served by helper(s)
- Catered by ______________________________

Gift List

Here's a handy place to keep track of all the gifts and services you receive at showers, ceremonies, or other celebrations. To make things especially easy, have a friend or family member record the gifts as you open them.

Gift/ Service	Given by	When and Where Received	Thank-You Sent

Chapter Eight

Childcare

What Kind of Care Should I Provide for My Baby?

The right childcare for your baby depends on your family's needs. You or your partner may choose to stay at home and provide the care yourself. Or you may plan to return to work full-time or part-time and arrange for childcare during your working hours. Each type of childcare has advantages and disadvantages. You must weigh the pros and cons of each before choosing the childcare that best ensures your baby's safety and well-being, meets your family's needs and budget, and gives you peace of mind.

Childcare Options

Formal or Licensed Daycare

Daycare Center
(publicly subsidized, privately owned, or affiliated with a house of worship)

Advantages

- Caregivers are supervised, and a director oversees the operation. In many centers, staff members are trained in early childhood education so they can nurture children's developing skills accordingly.
- Has clear rules for parents to follow (for example, pickup and drop-off times) so you know what's expected of you.
- Offers a structured environment and provides various activities throughout the day to teach children different skills.
- Gives your child the opportunity to socialize with other children.
- Can remain open even when some staff members take vacation or sick days.
- Offers parents the opportunity to form a support network with other parents.

Disadvantages

- Can be inflexible when scheduling problems arise. You may have to pay a hefty fee for late pickups, find backup care when the center closes for holidays, and keep your child home when he or she is sick.
- Because your child is constantly around the other children at the center, he or she is more likely to catch communicable illnesses, like colds and pinkeye.
- Staff members often can't provide the one-on-one attention your child needs.

Home Daycare
(also called *family* or *in-home* daycare)

Advantages

- Provides your child an environment similar to your own home.
- Many home daycare providers are parents of young children, so they're familiar with baby and childcare basics.
- Usually provides care for children of different ages, giving younger children the chance to socialize with older children.
- Tends to remain open for more holidays than most centers.
- May be more flexible about pickup and drop-off times and less likely than a center to charge you a costly fee when you're late.

Disadvantages

- While some states require home daycare providers to take basic health, childcare, and safety courses, few providers have formal childcare or early childhood education training.
- Depending on the state in which you live, licensing requirements may not be stringent or enforced.
- If your provider gets sick or takes a vacation, he or she may not arrange for a suitable substitute, leaving you scrambling for backup childcare.

Informal Daycare

Nanny

Advantages

- You don't have to deal with the policies of daycares or the politics of relative care.
- Your baby stays at home and can keep to his or her napping and feeding schedules.
- Your baby is exposed to fewer germs and may consequently contract fewer illnesses.
- Your baby will receive lots of one-on-one attention.
- If scheduling problems arise, a nanny can be very flexible.

Disadvantages

- Care is largely unsupervised, making it extremely important that you hire a nanny you trust.
- Should your nanny decide to leave, you'll have to find another or make other childcare arrangements.

- Your child won't have the opportunity to socialize with other children, unless you make arrangements.
- Is nearly always the most expensive childcare option. Families must pay the nanny wages (depending on where you live, they can be nearly quadruple that of minimum wage) and provide benefits, like medical insurance and paid vacation and holidays. If good nannies are in demand where you live, you may need to offer additional perks like a health club membership or personal phone line.
- You must handle tax requirements for employing a nanny. (See page 204 for more information.)

Share Care

(Two or more families share the expense of employing a nanny to care for their children.)

Advantages

- Helps parents build an extended family network. If your nanny gets sick or takes a vacation, more than one or two parents can be called upon to watch the children.
- Although the nanny will care for more than one child, your child is more likely to get one-on-one attention from him or her than from a daycare provider. This advantage is especially important for children under age one.
- Your child can socialize with the other children cared for by the nanny.
- Your child can stay in a familiar environment—his or her home or the home of a participating family.

Disadvantages

- Depending on those participating, share care may be the most complicated childcare option. You and the participating families must:
  - Make sure you share similar parenting philosophies on discipline, food, napping, and activities.
  - Agree on which nanny to hire, how much to pay him or her, and what benefits to offer. Write and sign a contract, and make sure to complete and file the proper paperwork.
  - Agree on ways to communicate with one another on all details, and be patient when you disagree.
- Care is largely unsupervised, making it extremely important that all participating families trust the nanny. Keep in mind that the nanny will be caring for more than one child.

Au Pair

(Au pairs are young foreign nationals who live with American families for up to a year. In exchange for room, board, a small stipend, and payment toward the cost of educational course work, they help with childcare and may do light housework.)

Advantages

- Using a reputable agency to hire an au pair better ensures that you'll find one who can provide your family many of the same services you'd get from a live-in nanny. Most agencies screen all candidates and accept only those with prior childcare experience and who speak English well, complete training, and have learned first aid and infant and child cardiopulmonary resuscitation (CPR).
- Because an au pair isn't considered a household employee, you won't have to pay taxes for his or her services as you would with a nanny.

Disadvantages

- Unlike most nannies, au pairs do not consider childcare their careers. Many au pairs take positions to experience a cultural exchange and may not appreciate their responsibilities as caregivers. While agencies strive to screen out applicants who don't fully understand what will be expected of them as au pairs, host families may still encounter problems with au pairs who don't understand their roles.
- While not as expensive as employing a nanny, a host family must provide the au pair with room, board, a weekly stipend, and payment toward the cost of educational course work, along with paying the agency a program fee and an application fee.
- Host families are expected to treat au pairs as family members, which can complicate the employer-employee relationship if rules aren't set and agreed upon by all.
- If you hire an au pair from an agency whose reputation isn't solid, you can't be sure of his or her competence. He or she may not have any previous experience caring for children, may not speak English well, and may not have any child safety training.
- Employment ends after one year, leaving you to make other childcare arrangements.

Relative Care

Advantages

- You can trust that your caregiver has your baby's happiness and well-being in mind.
- Your baby stays in a familiar environment—either your home or the relative's home.
- Your baby will receive maximum one-on-one attention.
- Is nearly always the least expensive option.

Disadvantages

- Is not regulated or licensed by any government agency or association.
- Being related to the caregiver can hinder establishing a firm employer-employee relationship, which can lead to other problems. For example:
  - The caregiver may dismiss your ideas on feeding, disciplining, and sleeping, thereby undermining your authority, confusing the child, and harming your relationship with the caregiver.
  - Tension can arise over the amount of childcare provided, or over compensation.
  - If the caregiver is older, he or she may not have the energy to safely care for your child.

Stay-at-Home Parenting

Full-Time At-Home Parent

Advantages

- The at-home parent is present during your child's prime developmental years, enhancing the physical and psychological well-being of the entire family.
- The at-home parent avoids the stress of juggling job responsibilities and family responsibilities.
- If the at-home parent is mom, breastfeeding is easier.

Disadvantages

- Stay-at-home parents may feel lonely, bored, and isolated from other adults. They may experience a loss of self-esteem and identity.
- You will need to make sure you provide your child a stimulating environment every day, including providing opportunities to socialize with other children.
- It's often less expensive for one parent to stay home than it is to pay for a nanny or daycare. But depending on your family's reliance on a second income, stay-at-home parenting may not be an affordable option.

Tag-Team At-Home Parents
(Parents stagger their work schedules and take turns at home.)

Advantages
- Both parents continue to earn income, which may reduce the financial strain of at-home parenting.
- Both parents continue to reap the social, intellectual, and professional rewards of working outside the home.
- Both parents are directly involved in their child's life.

Disadvantages
- Some tag-team parents still have to deal with daycare.
- Most tag-team parents must work harder to make time for each other and for the entire family to be together.

Childcare Cost Comparison

It's important to consider the cost of childcare as you plan a financial future that fits your growing family. How much of your budget will go toward childcare depends on a number of factors, including:
- Where you live
- The type of childcare you choose
- How many hours per week your baby spends in childcare

The following list ranks childcare options from typically most expensive to typically least expensive:
- Nanny care
- Daycare center
- Share care
- Au pair
- Home daycare
- Relative care
- Stay-at-home parenting

Keep in mind that many factors can affect childcare costs and that the preceding list may not apply to your circumstances. For example, in your area nannies may be in such high demand that share care is more expensive than a daycare center. Or you may consider the loss of income that comes with stay-at-home parenting an expense that's more costly than an au pair's wages.

How Do I Find a Good Daycare?

Steps to Follow

If you decide to use a daycare center or home daycare, follow these steps to find the best one for your baby. Be patient and prepared to visit many providers. This search may take a lot of time and energy, but don't settle for a less-than-perfect daycare. Remember: Your child deserves the best care you can find.

1. Know what you want. Are you looking for a daycare near your home or your work? Do you want your baby around lots of other kids or just a few? How much can you afford to pay? Will you need a lot of flexibility?

2. Broadcast your search and research your options. Ask friends, family, healthcare providers, coworkers, and houses of worship to help you find the most reputable daycares. Some employers offer childcare referral benefits; check with yours. Call the Childcare Aware hotline at 800-424-2246 to find the phone number of your local childcare resource and referral agency, which can refer you to licensed and accredited centers and home daycares in your area. (See page 193 for more on licensing and accreditation.) Check online resources, too. Visit http://www.naeyc.org or http://www.nafcc.org to find daycare guidelines and contact information. If all else fails, check the phone book. The yellow pages will list daycare centers and home daycares in your area.

   If a daycare sounds promising to you, note its name and phone number, the name of the person who referred it, his or her evaluation of it, and what he or she paid for its services.

3. Visit and interview daycares. (See page 185 for a list of interview questions.) You can ask basic questions over the phone (for example, about fees and available openings), but you won't know what a daycare is really like until you visit it. The more time you spend interviewing a potential daycare center or home daycare provider, the better. At each interview, note the name of the daycare, the name and position of the person you're interviewing, the daycare's address and phone number, and the date. Trust your intuition and pay close attention to how the center's staff or the home daycare provider answers your questions. After the interview, ask for a copy of policies and a schedule of the day's activities, then record your observations and impressions of the daycare.

4. Check references. Ask parents why they love a certain daycare. Nothing provides a ringing endorsement of a daycare like other parents' positive evaluations. Ask parents specific questions. Don't simply ask whether they *like* the center or provider; ask what exactly they like about the care and what they don't. Here are other good questions to ask:
   - How old are your kids, and how long have they been enrolled in the daycare?
   - If your children are no longer enrolled, why did you remove them?
   - How did you select the daycare?
   - How has the daycare helped you with normal developmental issues and concerns?
   - Have you had any problems with the daycare? How have you resolved differences?
   - Have your children ever been hurt in daycare or not wanted to attend daycare? What happened?
   - Have you had your children in other care? How do they compare?
   - What's the best feature about the daycare? Any weak points?

   For added assurance, call your state's Better Business Bureau to find out whether any complaints have been filed against the daycare.

5. Make an unscheduled visit. Dropping in unannounced can provide you with a more accurate picture of the daycare's day-to-day operations. Does the care seem as excellent as it did during your formal visit?

6. Visit the daycare with your child. See how he or she and the caregiver(s) interact. Does your child seem comfortable in the environment?

7. Get on the waiting list, if it's an option. If the perfect daycare doesn't have space for your child, securing a spot on the waiting list nearly always means that your child will get in—eventually. In the meantime, ask the daycare to recommend other similar places and arrange for other care (share care, relative care, or other) until a spot becomes available.

Daycare Center Staff Interview

Fundamentals and Philosophies

- When did the center open for business?
- Is the center licensed and inspected? Is the license current? Is the center accredited?
- How many children are enrolled? What's the age range?

- Is there a separate room for infants? How many babies are in the room (preferably six or fewer)?
- Is the infant-to-staff ratio no more than three to one? Will the same person care for my baby every day?
- How does the staff stimulate babies throughout the day? Will my baby be kept in a swing or bouncer seat? For how long? Will my baby be allowed on the floor? Is the floor padded? Is the floor cleaned daily?
- What's the daily schedule of activities? Does it include outdoor play? Does it include TV viewing? If so, how much?
- How does the staff respond to crying infants? How do they discipline disruptive children? What are some examples? How willing is the staff to follow my discipline guidelines?
- What does the center expect from parents?

Staff Qualifications

- What are the staff members' educational background, credentials, and training? How about interests, experience, or church or social affiliations?
- How are candidates for staff positions screened?
- Do all employees undergo federal background checks, including criminal and child abuse checks?
- Must employees pass regular physical examinations and have up-to-date vaccinations?
- Are staff members first-aid and CPR certified (including infant training)?
- How much is the staff paid? Any benefits?
- What is the staff turnover rate? What's the average term of employment? (Children need consistency and will form strong relationships with their caregivers.)
- Will I be notified if a new staff member takes over care of my baby? Can I request a particular staff member?
- Who can I regularly talk to about my baby's development, behavior, and needs? Will my baby's activities be recorded daily? Can I review the log?
- Are visits (expected and unexpected) from parents welcome?

Health and Safety

- What's the center's sick-child policy? What if the illness is minor? How will I be notified when my baby is ill?
- How often does the center experience outbreaks of serious contagious illness? How will I be notified of an outbreak?
- Does the center require a physical examination before accepting a child?
- Does it accept children who aren't vaccinated?
- Has a child ever been hurt while in the center's care? What happened?

- Has anyone pulled a child out of the center's care? If so, why?
- What is the policy on biting and other child-inflicted injuries?
- What's the protocol if a staff member suspects a child is being hurt at home or school?
- How does the staff manage children with allergies or special needs?
- Will my child's medical records and emergency information be posted in plain sight? Will the staff dispense prescription medications? Where will medications be stored?
- What safety measures does the center have set? Does it have a sign-in and sign-out sheet? Are the entrances monitored? What's the policy for having someone other than a parent pick up a child?
- Are fire extinguishers and smoke and carbon monoxide detectors present and in working order? Where are the fire exits? Are monthly fire drills performed?
- What's the cleaning schedule?
- Are cleaning products and other toxic substances locked out of children's reach?
- Are the food preparation and diaper changing areas sanitized frequently?
- How old are cribs, changing tables, and other equipment? How is the center notified of product recalls?
- Will babies have their own cribs? Can I bring toys and mobiles from home to decorate my baby's crib?
- How often does staff change linens? How are they laundered?
- Does the center have an enclosed play yard?
- Are the toys age-appropriate? How old are they and how often are they cleaned and replaced?
- Are staff members required to wash their hands after diapering and feeding each child?
- How often do they wash the children's hands?

Sleeping, Feeding, Diapering

- Can my baby be fed breast milk? How will breast milk be stored? Will my baby be held during feeding?
- Do you have a place for nursing moms to breastfeed?
- Is there a feeding schedule? A napping schedule? Will my feelings about scheduling be respected?
- Where and how often are diapers changed? How are diapers disposed? Is the center willing to use cloth diapers?

Fees and Operation

- What are the center's hours and holiday schedule?
- What's the policy for closing due to inclement weather?

- What are the fees for babies? Are the fees for older children less? How often are fees raised? Are there any additional fees? Will I be charged when I'm on vacation or my child is sick at home?
- Are pickup and drop-off times flexible?
- Will I be charged a late pickup fee? How much?
- How and when will I be billed?
- Will I need to provide supplies for my baby, like diapers and bottles?
- Will the center advise me of childcare tax credits and provide receipts?
- Is there an opening for my child? How do I apply?
- Is there a waiting list? How long a wait can I expect?
- Does the center give preference to siblings, if I choose to have more children?

References

- May I have a list of families I can call for references? (Make sure the list contains both families currently enrolled in the center and families no longer enrolled.)

Observations and Impressions

- Does the center have definite rules and regulations, a firm sick-child policy, emergency backup care plan, and staff members with solid, current credentials?
- Are the staff members' CPR and first-aid training adequate? Does the staff appear responsible, enthusiastic, and well prepared? Do they seem to share your philosophies on key parenting issues like sleep, discipline, and feeding?
- Is the staff-to-child ratio acceptable? (See page 194.) Does the staff appear to care for the children without difficulty? Keep in mind that an acceptable ratio is compromised if toddlers are always in the infant room, if a baby caregiver leaves to help with the toddlers, or if one of the babies has special needs.
- Do the staff and children seem happy and engaged? Is the general mood joyful and playful?
- Are the children under constant, attentive supervision?
- Do the staff members hold the babies? Talk and sing to them? Do they respond to crying babies immediately? When I ask them about individual children, do they seem to know each one and his or her needs and personality?
- Is the center inviting and clean? Clutter-free and organized? Does it seem overcrowded?
- Are the rooms adequately heated, air-conditioned, ventilated, and lighted? Are the food preparation, sleeping, eating, and changing areas impeccably clean? How about the restrooms?

- Is the center childproofed? (Open cupboards and crawl on the floor—your baby will.) Does the staff observe basic safety rules? Do you notice any safety problems like cords or tripping hazards? Do the crib sheets fit tightly (to reduce risk of sudden infant death syndrome or SIDS)? Is the play yard fenced in and away from streets?
- Is emergency information clearly posted? How about phone numbers for the police, fire department, and poison control? Where are the first-aid supplies located?
- Is the environment stimulating? Is the schedule of activities varied? Does TV play a minimal role?
- If the center serves meals and snacks, are they nutritious?
- What's the noise level? Is the napping area quiet? Is there background music?
- Does each infant have his or her own crib and cubby space (for pacifiers and other personal items)?
- Do the children's charts appear current, complete, and packed with detailed entries?
- Does the staff seem willing to listen to my concerns and happy to answer my questions?
- Will I feel at ease knowing my child is in this setting?

Home Daycare Provider Interview

Fundamentals and Philosophies

- When did you start your business?
- Do you care for your own children?
- How long do plan to stay in business?
- Are you licensed? Is the license current? Has your home been inspected as a daycare? Is your daycare accredited?
- How many children, especially babies, do you care for at one time?
- How will you stimulate my baby throughout the day? Will my baby be kept in a swing or bouncer seat? For how long? Will my baby be allowed on the floor? Is the floor padded? Is the floor cleaned daily?
- What's the daily schedule of activities? Does it include outdoor play? Does it include TV viewing? If so, how much?
- How do you respond to crying infants? How do you discipline disruptive children? What are some examples? How willing are you to follow my discipline guidelines?
- What do you expect from parents?

Provider Qualifications

- Why do you work with children? What do you like most about your job? What do you dislike?
- What childcare experience do you have? Do you have any formal early childhood development or childcare training? What are your interests and church or social affiliations?
- Do you have current CPR and first-aid training (including infant training)?
- Do you have any assistants? What are their credentials?
- If you don't have assistants, who covers for you when you're unavailable?
- Are visits (expected and unexpected) from parents welcome?

Health and Safety

- What's your sick-child policy? How will I be notified when my baby is ill?
- How often do you experience outbreaks of serious contagious illnesses among the children? How will I be notified of an outbreak?
- How often are your own children sick?
- Do you require a physical examination before accepting a child?
- Do you accept children who aren't vaccinated?
- Is your home childproofed?
- Has a child ever been hurt while in your care? What happened?
- Has anyone pulled a child out of your care? If so, why?
- What's your policy on biting and other child-inflicted injuries?
- Do you have any pets that will come into contact with my child? How long has the pet been in your home? Have any injuries been caused by the pet?
- What's the protocol if you suspect a child is being hurt at home or school?
- How do you manage children with allergies or special needs?
- Do you post children's medical records and emergency information in plain sight? Do you dispense prescription medications? Where will medications be stored?
- What safety measures have you set for your home? Do you have a sign-in and sign-out sheet? Are the entrances locked at all times?
- Do you receive personal visitors during the day?
- What's your policy for having someone other than a parent pick up a child?
- Are fire extinguishers and smoke and carbon monoxide detectors present and in working order? Are monthly fire drills performed?
- What's your cleaning schedule?
- Are cleaning products and other toxic substances locked out of children's reach?
- How old are cribs, changing tables, and other equipment? How are you notified of product recalls?

- Do babies have their own cribs? Can I bring toys and mobiles from home to decorate my baby's crib?
- How often do you change linens? How are they laundered?
- How often are food preparation and diaper changing areas sanitized?
- Do you have an enclosed play yard?
- Are the toys age-appropriate? How old are they and how often are they cleaned and replaced?
- Do you wash your hands after diapering and feeding each child?
- How often do you wash the children's hands?

Sleeping, Feeding, Diapering

- Can my baby be fed breast milk? How will breast milk be stored? Will my baby be held during feeding?
- Do you have a place for nursing moms to breastfeed?
- Do you provide meals and snacks or should I bring food for my child? What do you serve?
- Is there a feeding schedule? A napping schedule? Will my feelings about scheduling be respected?
- Where do the children sleep?
- Where and how often are diapers changed? How are diapers disposed? Are you willing to use cloth diapers?

Fees and Operation

- What are your hours and holiday schedule?
- What's your policy for closing due to inclement weather?
- What are the fees for babies? Do you charge less for older children? How often are fees raised? Are there any additional fees? Will I be charged when I'm on vacation or my child is sick at home?
- Are pickup and drop-off times flexible?
- Will I be charged a late pickup fee? How much?
- How and when will I be billed?
- Will you advise me of childcare tax credits and provide receipts?
- Will I need to provide supplies for my baby, like diapers and bottles?
- Is there an opening for my child? How do I apply?
- Is there a waiting list? How long a wait can I expect?
- Do you give preference to siblings, if I choose to have more children?

References

- May I have a list of families I can call for references? (Make sure the list contains both families currently enrolled and families no longer enrolled.)

Observations and Impressions

- Does the provider (and any assistants) have solid, current credentials? Does he or she have definite rules and regulations, a firm sick-child policy, and emergency backup care plan?
- Is the provider's (and any assistants') childcare background and CPR and first-aid training adequate? Does the provider appear responsible, enthusiastic, and well prepared? Does he or she seem to share your philosophies on key parenting issues like sleep, discipline, and feeding?
- Is the provider-to-child ratio acceptable? (See page 194.) Does he or she appear to care for the children without difficulty?
- Do the provider and children seem happy and engaged? Is the general mood joyful and playful?
- Are the children under constant, attentive supervision?
- Does the provider hold the babies? Talk and sing to them? Does he or she respond to crying babies immediately? When I ask about individual children, does the provider seem to know each one and his or her needs and personality?
- Is the home inviting and clean? Clutter-free and organized? Does it seem overcrowded?
- Are the rooms adequately heated, air-conditioned, ventilated, and lighted? Are the food preparation, sleeping, eating, and changing areas impeccably clean? How about the bathrooms?
- Is the home childproofed? (Open cupboards and crawl on the floor—your baby will.) Does the provider observe basic safety rules? Do you notice any safety problems like cords or tripping hazards? Do the crib sheets fit tightly (to reduce risk of SIDS)? Is the play yard fenced in and away from streets?
- Is emergency information clearly posted? How about phone numbers for the police, fire department, and poison control? Where are the first-aid supplies located?
- Is the environment stimulating? Is the schedule of activities varied? Does TV play a minimal role?
- If the provider serves meals and snacks, are they nutritious?
- What's the noise level? Is the napping area quiet? Is there background music?
- Does each infant have his or her own crib and cubby space (for pacifiers and other personal items)?
- Does the provider seem willing to listen to my concerns and happy to answer my questions?
- Will I feel at ease knowing my child is in this setting?

Daycare Licensing and Accreditation

Daycare Center

In most states, centers that care for more than twelve children must be licensed. A license, though, doesn't guarantee quality; it simply proves that a facility has met minimum state health, safety, and teacher training standards. How rigorous those minimum standards are depends on the state. Some states require only that a center be in satisfactory condition; others have stricter requirements. When considering a daycare center, ask to see its license to make sure it's not expired, then visit http://nrc.uchsc.edu/STATES/states.htm to learn your state's daycare center licensure regulations.

Accreditation is the gold standard of daycare quality. Accredited centers have met the stringent requirements issued by the National Association for the Education of Young Children (NAEYC). The accreditation process can take up to eighteen months, which is a main reason why very few licensed centers have earned accreditation. Visit http://www.naeyc.org to learn whether the NAEYC has accredited a center that interests you.

Home Daycare

Although technically most home daycares must meet state licensing standards for health and safety, many operate without a license, especially if the provider is caring for only one or two children besides his or her own. Many states require home daycare providers to submit to a background check and some training, but few states inspect all home daycares. (See the following section for more on background checks.) Some states simply require that providers mail self-certification forms to state licensing offices or add their names to a list. Visit http://nrc.uchsc.edu/ STATES/states.htm to learn your state's home daycare licensure regulations. Remember: a license doesn't guarantee quality care. Ask potential providers to show you their credentials, then call your local social services department to verify the information. If a provider is licensed, call your area's Better Business Bureau or your state licensing agency and ask whether any complaints have been made against the provider's business.

Because the accreditation process can take years, very few home daycares have been accredited by the NAEYC or the National Association of Family Child Care (NAFCC).

Background Checks

Check your yellow pages under *investigators* or *security* for companies you can pay to do child abuse, criminal, driving, credit, and social security or work authorization background checks on potential caregivers. You can also find such companies online; use the keywords *background check*.

Caregiver-to-Child Ratios

The ratio of caregivers to children can vary, depending on group size and state licensing requirements. (Visit http://nrc.uchsc.edu/STATES/states.htm to learn the caregiver-to-child ratios for your state.) The National Association for the Education of Young Children (NAEYC) has set these guidelines:

Daycare Centers

- For infants, the ratio is 1 caregiver for every 3 children if a group has 6 babies, 1 for every 4 if a group has 8 babies.
- For toddlers (age 12 to 24 months), the ratio is 1:3 for 6 children, 1:4 for 8 children, 1:5 for 10 children, and 1:4 for 12 children.
- For children between ages 24 and 36 months, the ratio should be 1:4 for a group of 8 children, 1:5 for a group of 10, and 1:6 for a group of 12.

Centers aren't required to follow NAEYC's guidelines, so ask what each center's ratio is and decide whether it's okay for you. A good center will keep the groups of children small regardless of staff size.

Home Daycares

The NAEYC recommends that a home daycare provider should care for no more than 2 babies (under age 30 months), 5 preschoolers (age 30 months to 5 years), and 2 school-age children (age 5 or older) at once.

Good Signs and Bad: The Top Six

Keep these important qualities in mind as you evaluate each daycare:

1. Reputation—good or lukewarm?
2. Rules and regulations—firm or loose?
3. Curriculum—stimulating or nonexistent?
4. Provider(s)—qualified and caring or unqualified?
5. Facilities—clean and safe or dirty and unsafe?
6. License—current or expired?

How Do I Find a Good Nanny?

Steps to Follow

If you decide to hire a nanny, follow these steps to find the best one for your family. Be patient, resourceful, and prepared for a long search. You may have to sift through dozens of applications and conduct several interviews, but don't settle for a less-than-perfect nanny. Remember: your child deserves the best caregiver you can find.

1. Know what you want. Do you want someone who's older and experienced? Is a nanny with a degree in early childhood education a priority? Make a list of qualities you want in a nanny. Refer to the list when you start interviewing applicants or talking to nanny agencies.

2. Broadcast your search and research your options. Ask friends and family to ask everyone they know for referrals. Post an ad in school newsletters, at local parenting resource centers, on online bulletin boards, and at local stores. You can advertise in a newspaper, but you may be overwhelmed with responses from less-than-ideal applicants. Record a message on your answering machine or voice mail asking applicants for names and numbers of their references. This way, you call around first and decide whom you want to interview.

   If there's a nanny training program in your area, call the organization for referrals. Or contact a local nanny placement agency, which screens candidates before agreeing to represent them, verifies work experience, often checks criminal and driving records, and may require blood and tuberculosis tests and a physician's statement declaring the nanny's good health. Be warned, though: An agency's search for candidates who meet your needs will save you time, but you'll pay several hundreds to several thousands of dollars for the service. You can visit websites like http://4nannies.com or http://www.nannynetwork.com to find some of the same services as nanny placement agencies, often without paying a hefty fee. Some also have useful guidelines and forms to help your search.

3. Write a job description that includes the information suggested by the list on page 198. Clearly defining the job now means spending less time settling disagreements later. Adapt the description as needed, usually once a year.

4. Interview nanny candidates. (See page 199 for a list of interview questions.) Talk to as many candidates as you can, and ask specific questions about work experience, parenting philosophies, personal habits and interests, and background. Before you start interviewing, make sure you've written a job description (page 198) and made a copy for each candidate to explain what you expect from the nanny. Start each interview by writing the nanny's name, phone number, and the date. Tell the candidate about your family and home, then share any positive qualities you've learned about the person to set a friendly tone. During the interview, trust your intuition and pay close attention to how the candidate answers your questions. After the interview, if the candidate seems promising, introduce him or her to your child. Watch how they interact and record your observations and impressions.

5. Check references. After you've selected a few promising candidates, it's important to call their references. Don't ask former employers whether they simply *liked* the nanny; ask them the following specific questions and note their answers in detail:
   - When and for how long did the nanny work for you? How did you hire him or her? Why did the nanny leave and with how much notice?
   - How many children did you have when the nanny started? Any infants? What gender and how old were they? What were the nanny's childcare and household responsibilities?
   - What was your general impression of the nanny? What did he or she do especially well? What tasks could he or she have done better? Any physical or emotional limitations? Anything you would change about him or her?
   - Did your children get along well with the nanny?
   - How did you and the nanny resolve disagreements? Did his or her personal life ever interfere with the job?
   - How would you describe the nanny's personality? Was he or she caring and warm? Patient? Respectful? Creative? Prompt and reliable? Did he or she have a positive attitude? Lots of energy? Sound judgment? Initiative?
   - How did the nanny handle emergencies? What's an example?
   - How did the nanny discipline your children? Did you ever suspect child abuse? Did you conduct a criminal, credit, driving, and child abuse background check?
   - Was the nanny generally healthy? How often was he or she ill or otherwise unable to work? Did you require the nanny to undergo a physical examination and TB test before hiring him or her? Did you ever suspect drug or alcohol abuse?
   - Was the nanny clean and well-groomed?

- Were the nanny's language skills satisfactory? Could he or she communicate easily with you? Read to your children? Did he or she keep a written record of your child's daily activities?
- How frequently did the nanny receive visitors? Make or receive phone calls? How much daily free time did he or she have? What did he or she usually do during that time?
- What was the nanny's schedule? Was he or she willing to be flexible? Were there other commitments?
- Would you use this nanny again?
- Would you mind sharing pay and benefit information?
- Any advice on ways to develop a good working relationship with this person? Anything else I should know about him or her? May I contact you again if I have additional questions?

6. Arrange for a tryout. Once you've narrowed your choices to a few candidates, schedule each separately to try out the job for a few days, ideally while you're still on parental leave. Pay each for his or her time and observe how he or she interacts with your baby. Before you take this step, complete the Childcare Organizer on page 202 and give a copy to the candidate. (If you also have older children that the nanny will be caring for, include instructions on discipline, TV, and other appropriate topics.) Seeing for yourself how a nanny follows your rules and respects your wishes is the best way to decide which nanny will work for you. Always trust your gut feeling and pay attention to all details.

7. When you've found the nanny you'd like to hire, consider drawing up a nanny contract. While a contract with your nanny isn't legally required—and is often difficult to enforce—it's still a good idea to have one. A contract spells out ground rules clearly and concisely. It also protects you and your nanny if problems arise; you can refer to it if you need to resolve a disagreement. If you like, have a lawyer review the contract after you've written it.

   The contract should cover everything connected to your nanny's job. If you've written a nanny job description (page 198), use it as a foundation for your contract. Add any additional applicable information—no detail is too small. Anticipate as many possible scenarios as you can and explain how you'll handle them. (For example, you might include a clause guaranteeing a pay percentage increase for every child added to the family.) At the very least, your contract should include the following information:
   - Weekly schedule (regular and overtime)
   - Childcare and household responsibilities and rules
   - Compensation and benefits

- Special considerations (for example, the time by which the nanny must call if he or she is ill and can't work)
- Emergency plans (for example, where the nanny should take the child if a problem arises and he or she can't care for your child before you return home)

You and the nanny should sign and date the contract. Make a copy of it for each of you. If minor changes must be made (for example, you agree to change the nanny's start time from 7:00 A.M. to 8:00 A.M.), you both should initial the amendments and each get a copy of the revised contract.

It's probably a good idea to include a clause that requires you and your nanny to reevaluate the contract on a certain date (like a work anniversary). At that time, you or your nanny can amend the agreement if appropriate. Keep in mind that if your household undergoes any major changes that aren't covered in the contract, you'll need to revise the agreement sooner than the scheduled evaluation date.

Nanny Job Description

A nanny job description should include the following information:

- Start date
- Weekly schedule (regular and overtime)
- Children's names, ages, special needs
- Parents' schedules
- Responsibilities
  - Childcare
  - Household
- Rules
  - Childcare
  - Household
- For live-in nannies
  - Location of living quarters
  - Rules
    - Privacy
    - Maintaining living quarters
    - Curfews
    - Overnight guests
    - Use of phone, TV, laundry, kitchen, computer, car, alcohol, and so on
    - Eating and traveling with the family
    - Other

- Compensation
  - Pay
    - Amount
    - Taxes withheld
    - Payday
    - Form of pay
    - Schedule of raises
    - Overtime rates
  - Benefits
    - Vacation
    - Paid holidays
    - Sick days
    - Bonuses
    - Car, laundry, phone, and/or computer privileges
    - Auto and/or health insurance

Nanny Interview

Background

- Why did you become a nanny? What do you think a baby needs from a caregiver? What's a nanny's role?
- Do you have any formal childcare or early childhood development training?
- Do you have CPR and first-aid training, including infant training? Are you certified? If not, are you willing to take classes if I pay for them?
- Where do you live and how long have you lived there? Do you plan to stay there?
- If you're not a U.S. citizen, what's your status? How long have you been living in America? Why did you leave your country of origin? How long do you plan to stay?
- Do you need to visit family outside this area? If so, how often and for how long?
- Do you have children? Who takes care of them? What about when they're ill?
- Do you speak any foreign languages? Play any sports? Swim? Have any special skills?
- What are your interests? What are your long-term goals?
- What do you think are your greatest strengths? In what areas do you think you could improve?

Experience and Approach to Care

- How long have you worked as a nanny? What do you like about the job? What don't you like about it?

- How many families have you worked for? How long did you work for each? How old were the children in your care? What were your responsibilities, pay and benefits, reasons for leaving? What did you like about working for them? What did you dislike? What rules worked well? What rules didn't?
- What about parents or children annoys or frustrates you? What do you do when you get annoyed or frustrated?
- What are your beliefs about raising children?
- What are your thoughts about putting babies on napping and feeding schedules?
- How do you discipline children? Do you believe spanking or hitting a child is ever necessary?
- How do you comfort children?
- What would you do with my child on a typical day? How much would TV play a role?

Childcare Situations

- What's an example of how you handled an emergency while caring for children?
- What would you do if my baby were ill? Hurt or bleeding? Choking? Unconscious?
- What would you do if, while bathing my baby, the doorbell rings and you know I'm expecting an important package?
- What would you do if my baby won't stop crying and you're at your wits' end?
- What's an example of a disagreement you had with a former employer? How was it resolved?

Logistics

- Will you expect live-in accommodations? If not, how will you get to and from work? If you drive, do you have backup transportation if your vehicle breaks down?
- How long have you had a driver's license? Any speeding tickets? Accidents? Do you have current auto insurance?
- Have you ever been arrested? If so, for what? Any other problems with the law?
- Will you submit to child abuse, criminal, driving, credit, and social security or work authorization background checks? (See page 193.)
- Do you have any health problems? How many sick days did you take in the last three years?
- Do you smoke?

- Do you have health insurance? When was your last physical examination? Last tuberculosis (TB) test? If the tests are more than a year old, will you agree to have a physical examination and TB test?
- Are you allergic to pets? How comfortable are you with them? Are you willing to help care for them?
- Are you comfortable answering the phone and taking messages? How about answering the door?
- Are you willing to do any household chores? Which ones?

Schedule

- Do you have any other commitments (family, jobs, church, school)? When are you available weekdays and weekends? Are you available overnight?
- Are you willing to take vacations with my family? Are you willing to take your vacation time while my family's on vacation?
- When can you start? Are you currently interviewing with other families? (If you meet someone you like and are flexible on the start date, let the candidate know.)

Expectations and Needs

- What qualities are you looking for in a family? What do you expect or need from the job?
- Do you need to receive visitors? Phone calls? Do you have any special dietary needs?
- Do you have any questions for me?

Observations and Impressions

- Was the candidate prompt for the interview?
- Did he or she seem attentive, competent, and reliable? Was his or her appearance neat and clean?
- Did the candidate communicate adequately? What did his or her body language tell me?
- Do the candidate's beliefs about childcare mesh with mine? Did he or she light up when talking about caring for other children?
- How did the candidate interact with my baby? Did he or she seem comfortable holding or speaking to my child? Did my child respond well to him or her?
- Will I feel at ease knowing my child is at home with this person?

References

- May I have a list of families I can call for references?

Childcare Organizer

Child's name: ______________________________

Feeding

What to feed: ______________________________
When to feed: ______________________________
Preparation instructions: ______________________________
Location of bottles and nipples: ______________________________
Location of bibs and burp cloths: ______________________________
Special feeding instructions (including choking hazards to avoid): __________
____
Nutrition guidelines: ______________________________

Safety

Location of
fire extinguisher: ______________________________
first-aid kit: ______________________________
circuit breaker: ______________________________
water shutoff valve: ______________________________
flashlights: ______________________________
Escape route directions and map: ______________________________

Sleep

Schedule: ______________________________
Naptime and bedtime routines and requirements (special blanket, music, and so on): ______________________________
Lights: ______________________________
Rules: ______________________________

Crying

Do not allow to cry for more than: ______________________________

Diapering

Schedule: ______________________________
Routine: ______________________________
Special changing instructions: ______________________________

Location of clean diapers: ____________________________
Disposal of soiled diapers: ____________________________
Supplies needed to clean baby: ____________________________
Location of clean clothing: ____________________________

Comfort Measures

Suggestions (place in bouncer seat, rock, offer pacifier, and so on): ________
____
____

Play

Favorite activities: ____________________________
____
Favorite places to go: ____________________________
Favorite toys: ____________________________
Favorite books: ____________________________

Visitors

Procedure for unknown or unexpected visitors: ____________________________
____
Personal visitors for caregiver: ____________________________

Special Needs and Medications

Description of special needs: ____________________________
____
Explanation of special procedures: ____________________________
____

Emergency Information

Parents' work numbers, pager numbers, cell phone numbers: ____________
____
Healthcare provider's name and number: ____________________________
____
Nearest relative's name and phone number: ____________________________
____
Neighbor's or friend's name and phone number: ____________________________
____
Poison control center: ____________________________

Police station: ______________________________
Fire station: ______________________________
Ambulance: ______________________________
Hospital: ______________________________
Veterinarian's name and phone number: ______________
Directions to home for emergency personnel: ______________
____

Medical Release Form

(This is a generic medical release form. Be sure to obtain release forms and all other recommended forms from your local hospital or hospitals.)

The emergency room of ______________ Hospital has my permission to treat my child, ______________,
for (list the care needed) ______________.
Our insurance company is ______________,
and the policy number is ______________.

____
Signature Date

The Nanny Tax

Paying the Nanny Tax

The nanny tax is a combination of federal and state taxes that an employer must pay the Internal Revenue Service (IRS) for employing a nanny. To legally employ a nanny, you must complete the following steps. Doing so will mean fewer complications for you and your nanny later on.

1. Get federal and state employer identification numbers. For the federal number, you must complete and return an SS-4 form. Visit http://www.irs.gov/formspubs/index.html to download a copy of this form or request one by calling the IRS at 800-829-3676. For your state number, look under *employment* in the state government listings in the phone book and call your state employment office for instructions.

2. Verify the nanny's eligibility to work in the United States. Visit http://uscis.gov/graphics/formsfee/forms/index.htm to download a copy of the Immigration and Naturalization Service (INS) Form I-9 or call the U.S. Bureau of Citizenship and Immigration Services (BCIS) at 800-375-5283 to request a

form. To complete the form, you'll need to see the nanny's passport or some combination of documents like a social security card, driver's license, birth certificate, green card, or work permit. Complete the form no later than the first day the nanny begins work. Make copies of the documents and file them for your records with the completed I-9 form.

3. Report new hires or rehires. Call your state employment office to learn about this procedure.

4. Establish a payroll system and pay taxes. You're responsible for paying your nanny's federal income taxes, social security tax, Medicare tax, state income taxes (in most states) and other fees.

   While you're not required to withhold income taxes from your nanny's paycheck, he or she will have to pay the taxes come April 15—and may owe penalties—if you don't. If you and your nanny decide that you'll withhold income taxes, he or she must complete a Form W-4 (Employee's Withholding Allowance Certificate) and determine filing status and how many exemptions he or she is taking. You'll need this information to figure out how much to deduct for the nanny's federal income taxes. File this form for your records.

   If your nanny is over age 18 and his or her yearly wages are at least $1,400 (tax year 2004), you must pay social security and Medicare taxes (FICA taxes). These taxes total 15.3 percent of your nanny's gross pay (tax year 2004). You may cover the full amount yourself or deduct half this amount from his or her wages. You may also be responsible for paying federal (and often state) unemployment taxes (FUTA taxes) and other applicable fees like Earned Income Credit (EIC) payments if your nanny gives you Form W-5 (Earned Income Credit Advance Payment Certificate). EIC is a tax credit for working, low-income people that can reduce the amount of federal tax they owe or result in a refund.

   To calculate how much to withhold for all these taxes, use an online tax calculator. Make sure your nanny's paycheck stubs list gross pay, all deductions, and the net amount of the check. File a Schedule H (Household Employment Taxes) form when you file your Form 1040. To avoid paying an interest penalty for underpaying these taxes, plan to pay the taxes quarterly, using Form 1040ES (Estimated Tax for Individuals). Call the IRS at 800-829-3676 for more information on making quarterly payments.

   By January 31, you must give your nanny copies of his or her Form W-2 (Wage and Tax Statement), detailing his or her wages and deductions for the previous year. File this form along with Form W-3 (Transmittal of Wage and Tax Statements) with the Social Security Administration by February 28.

5. Keep the following information in your records for at least four years:
   - Your state and federal employer identification numbers
   - Your nanny's name, address, and social security number
   - Dates of employment
   - Pay schedule and wages and taxes paid
   - Copies of all necessary forms (I-9, W-2, payroll tax returns, payment coupons for quarterly tax payments, and W-4, if used)
   - Dates and amounts of tax deposits (quarterly payments)

Resources

- For more information on your responsibilities as an employer and any federal forms you may need, view the IRS's Household Employer's Tax Guide at http://www.irs.ustreas.gov/irm/part4/ch22s12.html.
- For summaries of federal and state nanny tax requirements and links to many of the required forms, visit http://www.nannytax.com.
- For links to state tax departments for state forms and regulations, visit http://www.taxadmin.org/fta/link/forms.html.

Words to the Wise

If the task of paying nanny taxes overwhelms you, consult an accountant or a lawyer who specializes in labor law. Either can help you obtain the forms, talk you through the procedure, or handle the paperwork for you. You can also buy software that calculates taxes and prints paycheck stubs. Or you can sign up for a nanny payroll service. Use the keywords *nanny tax* to search for a list of vendors online.

Don't give in to the temptation to pay your nanny under the table—that's illegal. If the IRS finds out, you may have to pay any unpaid employer taxes, and you can't claim any childcare-related expenses on your taxes. You may even face prosecution. Plus, it's in your nanny's best interest to be paid legally. He or she will have a record of earnings (which are needed to apply for a credit card or loan) and be able to file for unemployment insurance, if necessary, and collect social security.

Are Nannies Licensed?

Unfortunately, no state procedures currently exist for licensing nannies. You must rely on other signs that a nanny takes his or her job seriously. Some attend institutions that train nannies, taking classes on first aid and cardiopulmonary resuscitation (CPR), child development, and nutrition.

Some have earned a degree in early childhood education. Keep in mind that while schooling and training are good qualifications (at the very least, a good nanny will know CPR and first-aid basics for infants), neither is a substitute for solid experience in caring for children.

Good Signs and Bad: The Top Seven

After you've hired a nanny, watch for these signs. If the nanny is providing the care you expect, great! If not, his or her performance may be grounds for dismissal.

Good Signs

- Your child is at ease with the nanny and enjoys being in his or her care.
- The nanny is considerate of your needs and respects your wishes.
- The nanny makes an effort to keep you informed of daily activities.
- Your child is clean, and his or her room is tidy.
- The nanny makes safety a priority; accidents are infrequent.
- If you have older children, they rave about all the wonderful things the nanny says and does, and they're eager to show off what the nanny has taught them.
- The nanny comes up with creative solutions to problems and works with you to provide the best possible care for your child.

Bad Signs

- Your child isn't happy to see the nanny and has become anxious and withdrawn.
- Your child has had frequent accidents while in the nanny's care.
- You notice the nanny isn't following your requests and instructions.
- The nanny often arrives late and often disrespects your wishes.
- Your child often looks unkempt and dirty.
- The phone is often busy when you call home.
- You suspect the nanny steals from, lies to, or deceives you in any way.

How Can I Make Share Care Work?

If you'd like to use a nanny but don't think your budget can handle the expense, share care may be a solution because you'll share the expense with one or more families. With share care, the nanny travels each day to one household or alternates if the families take turns hosting the children. Sometimes a nanny lives with one family and cares for the other families' children in that home. Share care can give you the best of both worlds: attentive care at a slightly cheaper price.

To find people interested in share care, talk to parents in your neighborhood who you think may find the arrangement appealing. If you haven't met many parents or are new to the area, post fliers at a local café, daycare center, gym, or baby store. Once you've found a few interested parents, make sure you share similar parenting philosophies on discipline, food, napping, and activities. Then follow the steps on pages 195–198 to find a nanny everyone likes. Make sure the share care arrangement is outlined clearly and concisely, so the nanny candidates understand exactly what the job entails.

Because more than two parties are involved in a share care arrangement, a detailed nanny contract is necessary as a reference in case problems arise. (See page 197.) The contract should include:

- How many hours each family agrees to pay for
- How taxes will be divided and filed
- The rate of pay and benefits
- Agreed-upon approaches to parenting

You and the other participants should pick one family to be the main contact in case anyone has to make scheduling changes. Plan to meet regularly so you all can discuss any problems with the arrangement. Agree on ways to communicate with one another on all details, and be patient when you disagree. For more information on share care, order a pamphlet from Bananas, a nonprofit childcare referral and support agency, by visiting http://www.bananasinc.org/purchasePubs.php.

How Do I Find a Good Au Pair?

If a nanny appeals to you, but you're wary of the cost and the potential hassle of finding a nanny who meets your needs and expectations, an au pair may be the perfect childcare option for your family.

Established in 1986, the Au Pair Program is an educational and cultural exchange program. Participants live with American families for up to one year and provide childcare while continuing their education. Although an au pair technically is an employee, the host family treats him or her as part of the family. Sponsoring agencies and organizations in the U.S. are responsible for managing the program, following the guidelines set by the U.S. Department of State (DOS). Although the DOS authorizes sponsors to manage au pair programs, their levels of involvement differ, and the host family and the au pair are responsible for choosing an agency or organization that fits their needs.

Most sponsors identify, screen, select, and match au pairs with host families. They make sure that au pairs undergo background checks, including criminal and child abuse, and that host parents have adequate financial resources to participate. They ensure that au pairs have all the training required by the DOS. Sponsors must monitor the au pair–host family relationship throughout the year, and local and regional counselors must contact au pairs and host families monthly to ensure compliance with the program.

After paying a sponsoring agency or organization an application fee and program fee, a host family typically must provide an au pair with a private bedroom, meals, payment based on the minimum wage, one and a half days off each week plus a full weekend off each month, two weeks' paid vacation, and the first five hundred dollars toward the costs of course work. Au pairs' duties must not exceed forty-five hours a week, and they're not responsible for household management. A host family needs to consider that the values and cultural perspectives of an au pair may be vastly different from theirs, which may lead to problems if neither party is prepared to reach common ground.

If an au pair sounds like a possible childcare option for your family, visit http://exchanges.state.gov/education/jexchanges/private/aupair.htm or call the DOS's Exchange Visitor Program at 202-401-9810 to learn more about the Au Pair Program. You can find several sponsoring agencies or organizations online. Au Pair in America (800-9AU-PAIR; http://www.aupairinamerica.com) or GreatAupair (925-361-0800; http://www.greataupair.com) are just two examples. Ask family members, friends, coworkers, and members of your house of worship or a social organization for the names and contact information of families who've employed or are employing au pairs. Ask these families to evaluate the sponsors they used and to comment on their relationship with the au pairs. Also ask them for any advice they may have on au pair childcare.

Comparison of Au Pairs and Nannies

Au Pair

- Is a young man or woman (typically age eighteen to twenty-six) with basic childcare experience
- Usually doesn't make a career out of childcare work
- Stays with a family for a cultural exchange and/or childcare work experience
- Term of employment is one year
- Is part of an exchange program and must be treated as a member of the family, not an employee

- Is required by the program to work no more than forty-five hours per week caring for children
- Is not required to do household chores or other domestic duties
- Is usually less expensive than a nanny
- Doesn't require payment of employment taxes

Nanny

- Is a man or woman who may be older than an au pair and usually has several years of childcare experience
- Often makes a career out of childcare work
- Stays with a family for a career-building experience, not necessarily for a cultural exchange
- Is employed for a term determined by the nanny or family
- Is considered a household employee (though may be treated as part of the family)
- Provides childcare each week for the amount of time the nanny and family agree upon
- Will do household chores and other domestic duties that the nanny and family agree upon
- Is usually more expensive than an au pair
- Requires payment of employment taxes

How Can I Make Relative Care Work?

If you're fortunate enough to have a relative who's willing to care for your baby, it's crucial to encourage open communication from the beginning. You're this person's employer, but you're also family, and the dual relationship can cause problems if you don't communicate your childcare expectations clearly and stay open to your relative's questions, comments, and concerns. Remember: This person is providing a valuable and (for many families) very inexpensive service, so make sure you recognize and appreciate his or her generosity.

Before a relative begins caring for your child, discuss the same issues you would with any caregiver, including parenting philosophies on discipline, feeding, napping, crying, and appropriate toys, activities, outings, and visitors. (It may be helpful to use the Nanny Job Description on page 198 as a guide.) Talk about work days and hours, time off, work location, compensation, and anything else that comes to mind. (No detail is too small.) Make sure you agree on a backup plan for when the relative is sick or otherwise unavailable. And don't forget to decide when and how often you and the relative will talk about the childcare arrangement. Having a chance to air worries and ideas is essential to making this relationship work.

If the idea of requiring a relative to sign a formal contract makes you uncomfortable, know that simply writing down the agreement may avoid problems later on. Some form of written agreement ensures that you and the relative understand what to expect from each other, and it becomes the impartial judge that you can refer to if problems arise.

Note: Depending on the relation of the caregiver to you, the amount you pay that person per year, and where the care takes place, you may be required to pay social security and Medicare taxes (FICA taxes) for the caregiver's services. Most parents using relative care don't have to worry about paying these taxes, but visit http://www.irs.gov to find out whether the Internal Revenue Service (IRS) considers your caregiver a household employee for whom you must pay FICA taxes.

How Can I Make Stay-at-Home Parenting Work?

When it comes to your baby's care, you may feel that no one can replace mom or dad. Staying at home with your baby can be rewarding, fulfilling, exciting, and even fun, but it's definitely not easy. The daily baby- and house-related chores and errands can be difficult to manage, as can the loss of income.

If you or your partner decides to stay at home with the baby, talk to other stay-at-home parents so you know what to expect. Analyze your financial situation to see whether your family's budget can support having a stay-at-home parent. (See page 146.) If stay-at-home parenting is possible for you, make adult interactions part of your daily schedule. Network with other stay-at-home parents, or moms and dads who work part-time. Keep in mind that it's essential for your baby's development—and your sanity—to get out of the house and let the world stimulate you both. If you keep meeting other parents at the park, consider starting a playgroup. Look for classes and activities for parents and babies. Many city recreation departments and community centers, local schools, and places of worship offer inexpensive "baby and me" classes or parents' groups. Also remember that it's important for you to schedule some time just for yourself each day—even ten minutes can help you reenergize and care for your child with a renewed spirit.

There are several stay-at-home parenting websites that can help you make this childcare option work. For example, visit http://www.familyandhome.org or http://www.slowlane.com/groups/homedadlink/index.htm to find information, tips, advice, and support for stay-at-home moms and dads. Books on the topic, like *Strategies for Stay-at-Home Parents* by Kristine Berggren, are other great resources.

How Do I Choose a Babysitter?

Steps to Follow

Whether you're planning to stay at home with your baby or you're returning to work and arranging for daycare, it's vital for parents to have an evening out alone every now and then. When you're ready to leave your baby in a babysitter's care, follow these steps to find the perfect babysitter for your family:

1. Start searching for a babysitter before your baby arrives. Ask friends, neighbors, relatives, other parents, and healthcare providers whether they know of any good candidates. Call the student employment service at a local college or high school and post fliers at gyms, youth centers, or places of worship. A baby-sitting agency is a good source for finding prescreened sitters (check your yellow pages for more information). You'll have to pay the agency for its services, but agency employees are usually older and more experienced than average teenage babysitters.

2. Interview candidates. (See page 214 for a list of interview questions.) Once you have a list of candidates, look for someone who you feel is old enough to do the job well. That person may be as young as age eleven, if he or she seems confident and knowledgeable about childcare. Most parents feel comfortable with a babysitter who's older (usually no younger than age fourteen), but you're the best judge of a babysitter's ability to care for your child. During the interview, trust your instincts and pay attention to how the candidate answers the questions. After the interview, if the candidate seems promising, introduce him or her to your child. Watch how they interact and record your observations and impressions.

3. Call references. After you've selected a few promising candidates, it's important to call their references. Don't ask former employers whether they simply *liked* the babysitter; ask them the following specific questions and note their answers in detail:
   - When and for how long did the babysitter work for you? How did you hire him or her?
   - How many children did you have when the babysitter started? Any infants? What gender and how old were they?
   - What was your general impression of the babysitter? What did he or she do especially well? What tasks could he or she have done better? Anything you would change about him or her?
   - How would you describe the babysitter's personality? Was he or she caring and warm? Patient? Respectful? Creative? Prompt and reliable? Did he or she have a positive attitude? Lots of energy? Sound judgment? Initiative?
   - Did your children get along well with the babysitter?
   - How did the babysitter handle emergencies? What's an example?
   - How did the babysitter discipline your children? Did you ever suspect child abuse? Did you conduct any background checks?
   - Was the babysitter clean and well-groomed?
   - Did the babysitter follow your rules and respect your home? Any problems with drinking, smoking, or unauthorized visitors?
   - Would you use this babysitter again?
   - Would you mind sharing pay information?
   - Any advice on ways to develop a good working relationship with this person? Anything else I should know about him or her? May I contact you again if I have additional questions?

4. Prepare for your babysitter. Before leaving your child in a babysitter's care for the first time, arrange for the babysitter to visit your home so he or she can get to know you, your home, and your child. You can ask him or her to arrive a half-hour or so before your scheduled departure. Or if you feel your babysitter doesn't have a lot experience caring for infants, you may want to pay him or her to drop by and care for your baby a few times while you're home. You can use the time to take care of other tasks, knowing that if problems arise, you're nearby.

   Give the babysitter as much information as you can, from emergency phone numbers (including the phone number of the place you'll be) to what food is off limits. See the Childcare Organizer on page 202 for more important information to include.

5. Maintain the relationship. Once you've established a good relationship with a babysitter, it's important to maintain it. Trusting a babysitter with your child should tell him or her a lot about how you feel about the relationship. The responsibility should make him or her want to do the best job possible. Tell your babysitter specifically what you've noticed that he or she does well. And always remember to treat your babysitter with respect. This may be his or her first real job, and he or she wants to be considered mature and capable.

Babysitter Interview

- How long have you been baby-sitting?
- Do you have experience caring for infants? Are you trained to perform CPR and first aid (including infant training)?
- Why do you like working with children?
- What do you like best about baby-sitting? What do you like the least?
- What other childcare experience do you have?
- Do you still baby-sit for your prior clients?
- What are the ages of other children you've watched?
- What activities do you enjoy doing with children?
- How do you soothe a crying baby?
- What's the best way to put a baby down to sleep?
- Have you ever given a baby a bath?
- If the babysitter will be transporting your child:
  - What kind of car do you have?
  - What's your driving record?
  - Do you know how to install and use a car seat?
- If the babysitter will be feeding your child:
  - How do you prepare a bottle (breast milk or formula)?
- If you have pets:
  - Are you allergic to any animals?
  - Are you comfortable around pets?
- What do you do in your spare time? Any hobbies? Other jobs?
- Do your parents support your baby-sitting jobs (if the babysitter is under age eighteen)? Will your parents be home while you're baby-sitting?
- Tell me about your school life. Sports? Activities? Grades? Do you like school?
- Will you need a ride to and from your house?
- How much per hour do you charge?
- May I have a list of families I can call for references?

Babysitter Pay Rates

Baby-sitting rates depend on many factors: where you live, how many children the babysitter will be watching, and the babysitter's experience, to name just a few. Hourly rates typically range from five to thirteen dollars, but you may need to pay more if good babysitters are in short supply. To get an idea of the current rate, ask neighbors and other parents how much they pay their babysitters. Your babysitter may set his or her own rates as well.

Baby-Sitting Co-ops

A baby-sitting co-op is several parents coming together and agreeing to take turns watching one another's children. A co-op assures you that your child will be cared for by the best kind of babysitter: another parent you trust. While you must commit the time to watch other members' kids, you can save money, especially if co-op members choose to compensate one another with baby-sitting time rather than money (for example, for every hour you baby-sit members' kids, you earn an hour of members' time to baby-sit your child).

To set up a co-op, talk to other parents in your neighborhood to find out whether the idea interests them. If you haven't met many parents or are new to the area, post fliers at a local café, daycare center, gym, or baby store. Once you've found a few interested parents, decide on guidelines together. For example:

- Should compensation be money or baby-sitting time?
- Should there be a quota system so members don't get taken advantage of?
- How should scheduling be handled?
- How should members who drop out of the group be handled (for example, if they owe or are owed baby-sitting time)?

Once the co-op has agreed on the guidelines, distribute a member list that includes each member's phone number(s), e-mail address(es), mailing address, and emergency contact information.

Chapter Nine

Final Countdown

Last-Minute Preparations

Your bag is packed, sibling care is planned, and you know how to get to the hospital. The following checklists will speed you on your way with the knowledge that you're truly organized!

Favors to Ask

Last-minute errands
Name(s) of possible helper(s): ________________________________

____

Care for baby's sibling(s)
Name(s) of possible helper(s): ________________________________

____

Check up on baby's sibling(s)
Name(s) of possible helper(s): ________________________________

____

Save the newspaper on the day of baby's birth
Name(s) of possible helper(s): ________________________________

____

Bring in your mail and newspaper
Name(s) of possible helper(s): ________________________________

____

Care for your family pet
Name(s) of possible helper(s): ________________________________

____

Call or e-mail extended group of friends and family with the good news
Name(s) of possible helper(s): ________________________________

____

Pick up printed birth announcements
Name(s) of possible helper(s): ________________________________

____

Help with special ceremony
Name(s) of possible helper(s): ________________________________

____

____

Help at home during first days postpartum
Name(s) of possible helper(s): ________________________________

____

____

____

Sibling Care Organizer

Before Labor Begins

- Notify daycare provider of alternate person(s) picking up child.
- Notify school of alternate person(s) picking up child.

If Labor Begins during the Day at Home

- Call ________________(name) at ____________(phone), who expects to:
  - ◇Pick up your child at your house.
  - ◇Pick up your child at school.
  - ◇Call school at ____(phone).
  - ◇Come to your house.
  - ◇Have you drop the child off at his or her house.
  - ◇Other plans: ____
    ____
    ____

If Labor Begins during the Day While at Work

- Call daycare provider or school at __________________________(phone).
- Call ________________(name) at ____________(phone), who expects to:
  - ◇Pick up your child at daycare.
  - ◇Pick up your child at school.
  - ◇Come to your house to pick up your child.
  - ◇Have you drop off your child at his or her house.
  - ◇Other plans: ____
    ____
    ____

If Labor Begins at Night

- Call ________________(name) at ____________(phone), who expects to:
  - ◇Pick up your child at your house and return to his or her house.
  - ◇Wait at home for you to drop off your child.
  - ◇Come over and spend the night at your house.
  - ◇Other plans: ____
    ____
    ____

If Sibling Will Stay Away from Home Overnight

- If appropriate, have your child sleep over at a friend's house before your baby's birth.
- Discuss with your child what to expect (waking up in another bed, different foods, wearing clothes packed in a suitcase, and different daily routine).
- Discuss how many nights your child may sleep away from home.
- Pack your child's suitcase with the following items:
  - Favorite blanket or stuffed toy
  - Small variety of other favorite toys, books, and so on
  - Photo of parents
  - Pajamas (two pairs)
  - Several changes of clothing
  - Diapers, if needed
  - Small gift from the newborn

Packing for the Hospital or Birth Center

For Use during Labor

- Camera, video camera, and/or audio recorder
- Personal comfort item(s) (pillows, flowers, pictures, music, and so on)
- Washcloth
- Rolling pin or tennis ball for back labor
- Birth ball
- Hot water bottle, heating pad, or hot sock
- Ice pack
- Warm socks
- Cornstarch, lotion, or massage oil
- Old nightgown or long T-shirt
- Childbirth book to refer to for ideas and information
- Swimsuit for partner (to accompany mom in shower or bath)
- Lip balm
- High-energy, easy-to-digest snacks
- Watch with second hand
- Paper and pen
- Birth plan
- List of important phone numbers
- Insurance information

For Postpartum

- 2 to 4 nightgowns or pajamas that allow easy access for nursing
- Robe
- Slippers, thongs, or other slip-on indoor footwear
- 2 to 4 nursing bras
- Nursing pads
- 4 to 6 underpants, both maternity and regular
- Going-home outfit (loose-fitting)
- 1 or 2 changes of clothes for partner
- Toiletries, cosmetics, and grooming items
- Cash (including coins) for parking, pay phone, vending machine, and/or other miscellaneous purchases
- Phone card
- Credit card
- Empty tote bag for extra take-home items
- Baby gear
  - Diapers
  - T-shirt or onesie
  - Sleeper or stretch suit
  - Socks or booties
  - Cap
  - Receiving blanket
  - Outdoors blanket, bunting, or other outerwear (must accommodate straps of baby's car safety seat)
  - Car seat (installed before labor)

Route Planner

Use the following planner for your trip to the hospital or birth center or to direct visitors. Include key information like street names, traffic lights, landmarks, and mileage. If you live in a large city, suggest an alternate route for rush hour. Finally, include a map showing the facility's location. (Request one from your hospital or birth center, or print one from an online map service such as Mapquest.)

From _______________ (starting point) **to** _________________ (facility name)

Directions: ____

____

____

Rush-hour directions: ____

____

____

From _______________ (starting point) **to** _________________ (facility name)

Directions: ____

____

____

Rush-hour directions: ____

____

____

From _______________ (starting point) **to** _________________ (facility name)

Directions: ____

____

____

Rush-hour directions: ____

____

____

Map

Early Labor Assessment

To help you decide when to call your caregiver and/or go to your hospital or birth center, check and track your symptoms using the following tools.

Signs of Labor

Type	Sign
Possible	Backache (vague, low, nagging, and/or intermittent) Cramps (menstrual-like, in lower abdomen) Soft bowel movements (several in several hours) Nesting urge (extraordinary burst of energy and/or desire to finish baby preparations)
Preliminary	Nonprogressing contractions (staying about the same length, strength, and frequency) Bloody show (blood-tinged mucus discharge from vagina) Amniotic fluid leak (small amount of watery discharge from vagina)
Positive	Progressing contractions (becoming longer, stronger, and/or closer together with time) Amniotic fluid gush (large amount of watery discharge from vagina) Dilation of cervix (confirmed by vaginal exam)

Early Labor Record

Contractions on: ________________ (date)

Starting Time	Duration (in seconds)	Frequency (minutes since beginning of last contraction)	Comments (on symptoms, activities, coping)

Quick Checklist for Emergency Birth

Sometimes labor progresses too rapidly for you to get to a hospital or birth center in time or for your caregiver to arrive for a home birth. In such an emergency, the following guidelines will help you achieve the best possible outcome. Review them now and keep a copy with you, just in case. Do these tasks yourself if you're alone. If you have a partner or helper with you, that person should assist you.

1. Get help if possible. Call your partner, your caregiver, your hospital or birth center, and/or 911.
2. Gather clean sheets, towels, paper towels, tissues, and extra clothing to be used during the birth and for your baby.
3. Wash your hands if possible.
4. Remove all clothing from your buttocks and vaginal area.
5. Lie down on your side or sit leaning back. Make sure you're in a clean place with enough room for your baby to land.
6. Put a sheet, towel, or some clothing under your buttocks.
7. Try not to hold your breath if your body is pushing. Pant through each contraction until your baby is born.
8. Wipe away mucus from your baby's nose and mouth.
9. Dry your baby's head and body.
10. Place your baby on your bare abdomen or chest.
11. Cover your baby using cloths, towels, or clothing.
12. Do not cut the cord.
13. Breastfeed your baby if possible.
14. If you're at home, await the birth of the placenta. (Place the placenta, still attached to the cord and your baby, nearby in a bowl, newspaper, or cloth.) If you're in a car, have someone else drive you and your baby to a hospital.
15. Place towels or a pad between your legs to absorb the blood flow.
16. Get medical help as soon as possible to check both you and your baby.

Chapter Ten

Postpartum Considerations

Life with Your New Baby

After you give birth, you'll discover a new world with your baby. The physical and emotional changes you'll experience, along with the increased responsibility, may leave you feeling overwhelmed. And the desire to do everything "right," from feeding and bathing your baby to keeping the toilets scrubbed, can only increase the pressure.

Don't feel you have to brave parenthood alone. Arranging for help and setting up a support system *before* your baby arrives will ensure that you can manage—and enjoy—the first few weeks with your little one. Think now about the kind of help you'll need. For example, you may want:

- Help with baby care, including breastfeeding, bathing, comforting, and so on
- Help with household tasks, like meal preparation and laundry
- Transportation to medical appointments, the grocery store or pharmacy, and so on
- Companionship

Ask for help whenever you need it; this isn't the time to be reserved. And always remember this advice: If someone offers you help, whether it's to watch the baby so you can take a quick shower or to drive you to the grocery store, *take the offer*!

At-Home Help Sources

Your Partner

Ideally, your partner will plan to stay home for at least a week or two after your baby arrives. Doing so will allow you both to bond with and learn to care for your baby. Your partner can also fix meals, manage household tasks, and take care of you.

Your partner may be able to take off even more time from work. Thanks to the Family and Medical Leave Act of 1993 (FMLA), many parents can stay home for at least a short time when they have a new child without losing ground at work. The FMLA requires certain employers to grant an eligible employee a twelve-week unpaid leave upon the birth or adoption of a child and to restore the employee to the same or an equivalent job at the end of the leave. For more information on the FMLA, contact the nearest office of the Wage and Hour Division, listed in most directories under *U.S. Government, Department of Labor*. Or hop online and visit http://www.dol.gov/esa/whd/fmla/.

Relative or Close Friend

If your partner can't stay home with you after your baby's birth, ask a relative or close friend to help you during those first few weeks. In fact, having this person's help even if your partner *can* take time off from work can be a godsend for you both. Not only can this person help care for you and the baby, he or she can also run errands, do chores, prepare meals—anything to keep your household running so you and your partner can concentrate on your new roles as parents.

Postpartum Doula

A postpartum doula (different from a birth doula) takes care of you and your home so you can focus on your baby. Call the National Association of Postpartum Care and Services, an association of postpartum doulas, at 800-453-6852 to help you locate a doula in your area.

Support Systems

Other Parents

Regularly airing your parenting concerns with fellow parents can help you relieve stress. Try to find a confidant who isn't judgmental or critical and who can provide helpful advice.

Parents' Groups

Joining a parents' group lets you find other parents who may feel the same anxieties as you. You can get advice and tips from members that may ease your parenting worries. You can find a group through your healthcare provider, clinic, community center, or house of worship. If you can't find a group in your area, start your own. Or go online and create a group with other parents.

Friends

Don't lose touch with your friends. They're sure to want to visit with you and your family. Their visits can provide a civilized break and some order in a newly frenzied world.

Healthcare Provider

If the help and support you receive from friends and family don't seem sufficient, make an appointment with your healthcare provider or with a healthcare professional you trust. He or she can direct you to resources for professional support.

Tips for Staying Sane

You're exhausted. Your breasts leak milk. You have trouble summoning the energy to eat, bathe, or choose an outfit to wear. Although you have little to no experience, you now must provide care, nourishment, safety, and stimulation to a newborn. Little wonder you feel so overwhelmed! Take comfort: You won't be the first parent to feel this way, and you'll soon get the hang of parenting. To help you adjust to your new role more easily, keep these tips in mind:

- *Get out of the house.* Getting out for just a short while can make the long days with your baby seem more manageable. Plus, the fresh air and change of scenery are good for both of you.
- *Set attainable goals.* Your goal may be to take a shower before the day is over, or it may be to pick up the clothes on your bedroom floor. Any achievement, no matter how small, is still an achievement and goes a long way toward making you feel that you have a handle on your life.
- *Lower your standards.* Revise your definition of *clean*. Ignore dirty laundry and grimy surfaces longer than you did before your baby arrived. Be happy that you're able to shampoo your hair, even if you don't have a chance to style it properly.
- *Seize time to rest.* When your baby sleeps, you should sleep. Even if you can't sleep, use the time to rest, read, or simply daydream. Pass the time doing something that has nothing to do with the baby or housework. It'll be difficult to resist the temptation to get things done, but it's critical to have some downtime!

Symptoms of Emotional Distress

After childbirth, you'll experience emotional ups and downs. For some women, these emotional fluctuations are mild and subside within a few weeks. For others, they're overwhelming, long-lasting, and may require treatment. What are considered "normal" baby blues and what are the symptoms of postpartum mood disorders (PPMDs) and postpartum psychosis?

Baby Blues

Baby blues are temporary and rarely last longer than a week. Signs may include:

- Crying easily
- Feeling overwhelmed
- Feeling a loss of control
- Feeling exhausted, anxious, or sad
- Feeling a lack of confidence about being a parent

PPMDs

PPMDs occur within the first year after giving birth and can be long-lasting and require treatment. There four different emotional conditions with their own signs:

Postpartum Anxiety and Panic Disorder

- Shortness of breath
- Sensations of choking
- Lightheadedness
- Faintness
- Rapid heart rate
- Chest pain
- Immobilizing fear of being alone, of dying, of baby dying
- Fear of leaving home

Postpartum Obsessive-Compulsive Disorder

- Repeated, uncontrollable thoughts, speech, and rituals that interfere with normal daily living

Postpartum Depression

- Feelings of hopelessness, exhaustion, inadequacy, and low self-esteem
- Loss of interest in everything
- Angry outbursts
- Thoughts of harming self or baby
- Sleeplessness
- Forgetting to eat or overeating
- Constant crying

Postpartum Posttraumatic Stress Disorder

- Flashbacks
- Recurrent nightmares
- Rage
- Extreme protectiveness
- Anxiety
- Panic attacks

Postpartum Psychosis

Postpartum psychosis is rare. Its signs may include:

- Severe agitation
- Mood swings
- Depression
- Delusions

Thanking Your Helpers

Don't forget to thank your helpers while they're helping you and after you no longer need their help. They've given you their time and may have put their own lives on hold. Make sure you show them your appreciation.

After Your Helpers Go Home

Once you're ready to fly solo as a parent, sending each helper a heartfelt thank-you note is essential. Sending flowers or inviting them to dinner (you'll do the cooking or pick up the check) may also be an appropriate way to thank your helpers. Here are some other gift ideas:

- *Tickets*: If you're too busy to buy tickets at the box office, you can often buy them over the phone or online. Consider buying tickets for a:
  - Theater performance
  - Movie
  - Sporting event
  - Music concert

- *Gift certificates*: If you aren't able to buy gift certificates in person, you can often buy them over the phone or online. Consider buying gift certificates to a:
  - Restaurant
  - Movie theater
  - Live theater
  - Retail store (department store, sporting goods store, bookstore, and so on)
  - Online retailer
  - Spa or salon

While Your Helpers Are Caring for You

During early postpartum, many new parents and their helpers need space. Plan time-outs for your helpers, who will probably welcome the chance to get out of the house. Consider the preceding list of gift ideas for ways to give your helpers a break. Offering a gift not only shows your appreciation, but also gives your new family a chance to be alone. Be sure to provide a detailed map if your helpers are unfamiliar with the area. Here some other activities to consider:

- *Arrange an evening out with mutual friends.* Perhaps another friend could invite your helpers over for dinner or cocktails.
- *Prepare a list of local tourist activities or special events.* Buy tickets beforehand when possible.

Birth Announcements

After your bundle of joy has arrived, you'll want to let everyone know. You may want to send announcements by surface mail or e-mail. You may even decide to design a birth announcement website. Do as much preparation as you can now so you can send the announcements promptly. For example, preaddress and stamp the envelopes. Gather all the e-mail addresses you'll need. Build the website so it's ready to upload photos and text. Whatever way you choose to announce your baby's birth, be sure to include the following information:

- Baby's name
- Date and time of birth
- Baby's birth weight
- Baby's length at birth